BATH

KIRSTEN ELLIOTT | NEILL MENNEER

FRANCES LINCOLN

BATH

KIRSTEN ELLIOTT | NEILL MENNEER

Frances Lincoln Limited
4 Torriano Mews
Torriano Avenue
London NW5 2RZ
www.franceslincoln.com

British Library Cataloguing in Publication Data
A catalogue record for this book is available
from the British Library

ISBN 978-0-7112-2266-3

Printed in Singapore

2 4 6 8 9 7 5 3

INTRODUCTION

In 1687 that indefatigable traveller Celia Fiennes complained that all roads into Bath were steep and difficult. Today the roads have been improved, but from north and south visitors still make a lengthy winding descent into the valley. As they do so, they catch their first glimpse of Bath: the houses, built of the local limestone, the glint of light on the river, and at the city's heart, the Abbey, golden in summer sunshine. Or perhaps, in winter, when the fields are white with frost, the first impressions will be of honey-coloured terraces clinging to the hillside, with cold blue shadows between them where the warming sun cannot penetrate.

At night the view can be spectacular. 'In the midst of darkness, hundreds of enchanted palaces appear, one placed higher than another, until the highest seems to touch the dark azure vault,' raved A.B. Granville, a dedicated spa enthusiast, in 1841. Some even prefer Bath in the rain. Jane Austen complained that her first view of Bath in fine weather proved disappointing. 'The sun was got behind everything,' she wrote to her sister, Cassandra, 'and the appearance of the place from the top of Kingsdown was all vapour, shadow, smoke and confusion.'

For the first Roman visitors, arriving in the autumn of AD 43, weary after a long march over the hills, there were no buildings, no welcoming inns, no smoke and confusion. They were soldiers, part of the invading Roman army, pushing forward the boundaries of the Empire. They would have scrambled down the wooded slopes, taking wary glances through gaps in the trees as they descended. Only the clank and rattle of their armour and the sharp warning cries of startled birds would have broken the silence. They would have caught sight of the great bend of the river, with low-lying, marshy ground on its northern side. From the valley verdant slopes rose at first gently and then steeply. Amid the tangled briars and vegetation of the marsh loomed a dark stand of trees. This, their spies and informants would have told them, was the prize worth seizing. The Roman soldiers, their heads full of stories of the magic of the Druids, and their souls in the care of myriad gods from across the Empire, must have gazed on it with a mixture of awe and eager anticipation. For at its heart was a secret guarded by a deity, Sulis, attended by a mysterious priesthood. Clouds of steam drifting among the dark shadows of the sacred grove led devotees to the holy of holies, where, bubbling up from rust-red rocks and gravel, were the hot springs.

It is the presence of these springs which has continued to draw visitors throughout two millennia. They have come seeking health, religious inspiration, fortune, love, marriage, or simply pleasure. Bath has done its best to supply their needs. With the reopening of spa facilities come hopes of

LEFT A rural scene scarcely a mile from the centre of the city. Here the vista is westwards, down the valley of the River Avon, with the clump of trees on top of Kelston Hill visible in the far distance.

another revitalization of the city. The modern city offers its visitors a range of attractions: museums, restaurants and guided tours of all descriptions. Buskers vie with shops and street sellers to part the tourist from his money. As in past ages, there is accommodation to suit every purse. And as the tourists stroll through narrow lanes or promenade along wide pavements, the past is all around them – everywhere, beneath their feet, in the buildings, within the very fabric of the walls. The ghosts of bygone visitors, rich and poor, jostle their modern counterparts in an effort to tell their stories. The developers and architects of the eighteenth century have their memorial around them, in the terraces, squares and crescents, which together blend into something so special that UNESCO has designated it a World Heritage Site. There is also the other history which can so easily be forgotten: the lives not only of the working people, with their crafts and customs, but also of the desperately poor, whose only hope was parish relief and the charity of strangers. They too have a tale to tell.

Reader, when you come to Bath, cherish your first impressions. Write them down for future generations, as so many have done before you. Meanwhile, within these pages, with words and pictures, we take you behind the façade, and reveal the story of a little Somerset town that has become a world-famous city – BATH.

WATER IS BEST
THE HEART OF THE CITY

WATER IS BEST

THE HEART OF THE CITY

Bath lies not just in a river valley, but in an encircling bowl of hills, a point noted by almost every writer who has ever visited the city, from John Leland in 1540 to Jan Morris in 1982. Unseen by any visitors, however, because it lies deep beneath their feet, is another bowl: a layer of carboniferous limestone. It forms an elliptical dish stretching westwards along the valley of the River Avon, north into Gloucestershire, and south-west to the Mendip Hills, with Bath on its eastern rim. At its deepest point it is about two miles deep. The rocks are full of tiny fissures, and when rain falls it begins to percolate down through these micro-crevasses. For a period of between five and ten thousand years it has seeped through the geological strata, its chemical content changing, and its temperature rising to as high as 85°C as it approaches the centre of the earth. This much most geologists agree on. But then comes the mystery. It suddenly rises to ground level, and no one is really sure why. Professor Barry Cunliffe suggests this is caused by a fault line, but fault lines exist at other places. Another theory is that there is some subtle change in the structure of the rocks. Whatever the reason, the hot waters surface at a unique place – Bath. Without the springs there would certainly be no city; it is doubtful if there would have been any settlement here at all, beyond a few houses around a river crossing. Everything that can be seen and enjoyed in this vibrant city – the architecture,

the theatre, the festivals, the universities, the thriving shops and restaurants – exists because of a geological accident.

It is the springs that have attracted visitors to this valley for over seven thousand years. First to arrive, some time around 5000 BC, were Stone Age hunters, drawn by the warmth of the waters. If we, with all our technology, cannot comprehend why the water is hot, imagine how mysterious it must have seemed to them as, amid clouds of steam, they watched this perpetual outflow among the brambles and undergrowth of the marsh. Everything around the source would have been stained a deep rust red. Perhaps it was by accident that they left flint tools here, or perhaps the tools were the very first offerings to the guardian deity.

By the Iron Age this goddess was known as Sulis. Five thousand years after Stone Age man first overwintered here, camping among the springs, a ring of hilltop settlements had developed, encircling the valley, with scattered farmsteads on the lower slopes. Iron Age Britain was not a lonely, wild place, but heavily populated and tamed by people who lived in comfortable if simple dwellings, grew wheat and kept sheep. They spun wool and wove cloth, a trade that was to support Bath right into Tudor times. They ate and drank from crockery made of decorated pottery and used spoons made of bronze, all of which they paid for with coinage. They traded with Europe and for this they built trade routes

ABOVE After the major archaeological discoveries in the 1870s, an extension to the Pump Room was built in 1894 to protect the baths beneath, the carving above indicating the entrance to Roman Bath.

and tracks all over the country. Many of our so-called Roman roads, including the Fosse Way, which takes in Bath in its passage from modern Exeter to Lincoln, are old trackways adopted and modernized by the Romans.

A local legend even states that it was a Celtic prince, Bladud, who founded the first city. His statue sits in a niche above the King's Bath, and his strange story continues to fascinate people even today. This is the tale.

Once upon a time, nearly three thousand years ago, there was a prince called Bladud, the son of the British king Lud Hudibras. Somehow he contracted the disease of leprosy, and he was banished from the court to stop the disease spreading. The Queen gave her son a ring so that, should he ever be cured, he could prove his identity. Wandering the countryside, disguised as a peasant, he met a swineherd who offered him work guarding pigs. Alas, the pigs soon caught the dreadful disease. Bladud, anxious to hide the bad news from his master for as long as possible, drove the pigs alongside the river which we now call the Avon. At last they came to the valley where now lies the city of Bath, and they came upon the hot springs. Here the pigs rolled in the warm oozy mud. They were so enjoying themselves that they refused to come out, and Bladud had to lure them out with a trail of acorns, a food which pigs adore. As he washed and fed them he noticed that the pigs were losing all traces of the

disease, and the thought occurred to him that this might be a consequence of their dip in the hot springs.

Immediately he realized what he must do. He plunged naked into the hot waters and after a few days both he and the pigs were completely cured. After returning the pigs to the swineherd and telling him what had happened, Bladud, still disguised, returned to the court. He managed to slip the Queen's ring into her glass of wine and when she discovered it she cried out 'Where is my son?' He revealed himself to her and was received back with great joy.

For many years he travelled abroad, learning the arts of good government. When his father died he became king and it was then, in the year 863 BC, that he built cisterns for the hot springs, palaces and a new city which he called Caerbren. He also rewarded the swineherd with a large estate. It became known as Hogs' Norton, in memory of the pigs, but the swineherd, feeling it was too small a reward for his kindness, gave it another name, the one it still bears today, Norton Malreward.

The story of Bladud does not have a happy ending. All his learning had convinced him he had the ability to fly. Having built a pair of wings he tried out this theory but, to the dismay of the watching populace, he crashed to his death. However, he still lives on – in the street name Bladud Buildings, in the memory of local people, in the name of a

ABOVE The Victorian design included statues such as this one, gazing down on the Great Bath and across to the Abbey.

pub, in the trademark of a publishing company, and on one or two very strange websites. He is also the inspiration for an annual poetry competition, the Bard of Bath, organized by the Bladud Society. The competition, like this story, is not to be taken too seriously.

Beguiling as the story is, the facts are rather different. We do not know for certain if the local tribe, the Dobunni, built close to the springs but it is thought that they held back, to preserve the mystery and majesty. They did, however, construct a causeway into the centre of the biggest pool, where offerings of silver and gold could be made to the goddess. Almost certainly, the area was hidden by a sacred grove. Even the Romans, sophisticated as they were, found these groves intimidating places. Their army, made up of different peoples of the Empire, all with their own gods, must have been very fearful when in AD 43 they first marched over the hills and saw what lay below.

Fear can spur men to violence. In addition to the superstitious fears the mysterious mist-enshrouded morass must have aroused, the Romans well knew that the British were a warlike nation whose courage had caused even the great Julius Caesar to retreat from their island shores nearly a century earlier. It appears that, when they took possession of the area around the springs, the soldiers pushed a military road right through the most sacred part of the site, in an act

designed to humiliate and subdue the local people. They also established a military camp somewhere in the valley, possibly near modern Bathwick. For fifteen years the Roman tactics worked. But in AD 60 the Iceni, in south-east Britain, decided they had suffered enough. Led by their charismatic queen, Boudicca, they rebelled against the Romans. It was a savage, bloody revolution, and it was put down with savagery, but not before three towns, including London, had been burnt to the ground. Insurrections broke out even in the far south-west. The Roman grip on Britain had very nearly been broken.

The Roman administration had to think again, and find diplomatic ways to pacify this proud people. It appears that as one act of conciliation the springs were enshrined once more as a holy place, this time dedicated to a goddess who was an amalgam of the Roman Minerva and the Celtic goddess of the waters, Sulis. The town which grew up around the temple precinct was also given a Romano-British name – Aquae Sulis, the waters of Sulis. It may even have been a Romano-British client king, Tiberius Claudius Togidubnus, who was the backer of the project. As a Romanized Briton and ally of the Empire, he was regarded as a traitor by many of his fellow countrymen, and it might have been to show neighbouring tribes the benefits of the Roman occupation that he embarked on the scheme.

LEFT With the water in the King's Bath lowered to the Roman level, the stone ledge and rings for weary bathers can be seen. The high iron content of the water causes the brown coloration of the stone.

BELOW Bladud, legendary founder of the city, presides over the King's Bath.

OPPOSITE Known as the Gorgon's Head, this striking carving which formed the centrepiece of the temple pediment may well represent the sun god. The temple faced east, and the carving would have glowed red as the sun rose.

BELOW The outflow from the Sacred Spring. This archway with its cascade may have been built to impress visitors, or may simply be a relieving arch in the reservoir wall.

Our ideas of what Aquae Sulis was like, and how large it was, are constantly being updated. Archaeology is a hit and miss science. The archaeologists are often limited in their choice of sites, and trying to build a clear picture of a location can be like struggling with a jigsaw puzzle that has most of the bits missing. From time to time a few more pieces turn up, and the overall picture alters. This is what has happened in Bath.

By far the biggest area to have been archaeologically explored is the Roman baths, but long before their discovery it was well known that Bath was a Roman city. When John Leland came, in about 1540, he remarked upon the carved stones and inscriptions which he could see in the city wall. He also noted, perceptively, that there were local elements within the carvings and that the stones had been taken from somewhere else and put in the wall. Over the following centuries, discoveries during building, including a tessellated pavement uncovered by the architect John Wood, prepared local people for the first discovery of the Roman baths in 1755, when the Duke of Kingston was building a new suite of private baths south of the Abbey. There were further finds in 1790, when work was being carried out on the Pump Room, but it was not until 1871, when the City Engineer, Major Davis, was called to solve the problem of a leak in the King's Bath, that the archaeologists began to grasp some idea of the size of the Roman bathing establishment some six metres below the level of the present city. Explorations of this and other Roman sites in Bath continue to the present day.

In descending the stairs that lead to the Roman Baths Museum, the visitor is also making a journey back in time – to the central part of Aquae Sulis. Before descending, the visitor looks down on the Great Bath, 22 metres long, 8.8. metres wide and 1.5 metres deep. This is very close to the measurements of the main pool in the modern sports centre, and is our first intimation that some surprising similarities between old and new may be discovered during the visit. Human nature has changed little over the centuries, and the museum shows that the citizens and visitors in Aquae Sulis loved and hated, enjoyed life's little luxuries and worried about life's problems in very much the same way that we do. A wide variety of items, from coins to curses, from gems to tombstones, give an insight into their daily lives.

Arriving at the temple precinct, the visitor comes to the earliest part of the development. The Romans tamed the largest spring (which is now referred to as the Sacred Spring) and encircled it with a reservoir. The temple and first suite of baths were built by the late first century. The temple, of which virtually nothing remains but a few columns and the dramatic pediment, was dedicated to the Celtic goddess Sulis and the Roman goddess Minerva. Within the pediment was the carving which has become the symbol of the Roman baths, the Gorgon's Head. With its face surrounded by writhing snakes and its piercing eyes, it is a fearsome, vigorous image, which must have struck terror into the hearts of some of the less sophisticated visitors to the temple. Previously it was thought that it was almost certainly carved by a local stonemason who was unaware that Medusa was a woman, but recent writers, including Professor Cunliffe in his book *Roman Bath Discovered*, have suggested that images of other gods, such as the sea god Oceanus or the sun god Sol, may have influenced the sculptor. Since another building in the temple courtyard showed the moon goddess Luna, it seems highly likely that there would also have been a representation of Sol.

Within the temple stood the statue of Minerva. All that has ever been found is the head, discovered while workmen were digging in Stall Street, just where the temple stood. Almost certainly the statue was overthrown and the head hacked from the body when Christianity became the official religion of the Empire in AD 391. Research has shown that there were at least four layers of gilding on this head. It seems probable that there were so many layers because the gilding was worn away by frequent polishing necessary not only because the temple was lit by smoky oil lamps but also because votive fires, fuelled by Somerset coal, caused soot to gather on the statue.

While the Great Bath dates from this early period, the two suites of baths to east and west are part of later expansions. During the second century a more elaborate set of heated rooms replaced the warm pool at the eastern end, while cold plunges and saunas were added at the western end. Throughout the remaining years of the Roman occupation, further changes were made to keep in line with fashion and Imperial decree. In the second century, for example, Hadrian banned mixed bathing. Some baths in other parts of the Empire then had to have different opening times for men and women, but at sophisticated Aquae Sulis new, separate suites of baths allowed men and women to visit at the same time.

Bathing was not just a self-gratifying experience – the proximity of the temple and the offerings which have been

LEFT Steam rises from the Great Bath, which was kept at a pleasantly relaxing temperature. The overflow from the Sacred Spring drained under the raised stone in the foreground through a lead conduit into the lead-lined Great Bath.

RIGHT The late-nineteenth-century building to protect the baths left the Great Bath open to the sky. In Roman times it was covered, first by a timber roof and then by a vault constructed of brick and tiles.

ABOVE Items from the Roman Baths Museum. Left to right: A carved stone showing a man with a dog pursuing a hare; a carving of three mother goddesses, found near Bathwick Hill; the tombstone of cavalryman Lucius Vitellius Tancinus, who at the age of forty-six died in Aquae Sulis, far from his native Spain; the head of Sulis Minerva, discovered beneath Stall Street in 1727 – the rest of the gilded statue has never been found.

OPPOSITE The Great Bath at night. Part of the temple complex lies, still unexplored, beneath Bath Abbey, which can be seen behind the baths. The 'treatment' baths, with their extremes of hot and cold, are to east and west of the Great Bath.

discovered in the drain show that it was closely associated with religion. However, the bathers also had pleasure in mind. Having enjoyed the various hot and cold plunges, the steam rooms and the saunas, they could relax in and around the Great Bath, while musicians, masseurs, barbers and fast-food outlets vied for their custom.

Outside the immediate vicinity of the baths, our knowledge of the city is more conjectural. Quieter, less elaborate bathing establishments seem to have been built around what today we call the Cross Bath and the Hot Bath. Almost certainly there would have been a theatre, and perhaps smaller temples to other deities.

The picture is complicated by an encircling rampart, later the basis for the town wall. Did this mark the full extent of the city? It is now thought that in Roman times it was the boundary of the religious and administrative area, which included the temple complex, the bathing establishment, and other public buildings as yet undiscovered. Outside the rampart a thriving market town grew up. We know something of the people of that town by the relics they left behind. Tombstones have been discovered along the roadsides leading out of Bath. One is that of Gaius Calpurnius Receptus, a priest to the goddess Sulis, who was seventy-five years old when he died. Nothing unusual in that, perhaps, but this high-caste priest was married to a freed slave. Another freedwoman

was Mercatilla, the foster daughter of Manius. Sadly, she did not live long enough to enjoy her good fortune. The tombstone tells us her precise age: 1 year, 6 months, 12 days. We know no more about her. Why was she freed so young, and why was she adopted by Manius? Behind the simple inscription lies a story we can only guess at.

It seems that the people of Aquae Sulis were often angry with their fellow citizens, and among the offerings to Sulis Minerva are curses, scribbled on lead sheets, rolled up and thrown into the spring. The goddess Minerva was requested to bring terrible vengeance on the perpetrators of various crimes, most often theft of personal items. To help her, she was sometimes supplied with a list of suspects. Some are written backwards – whether to make the curse more secret or more powerful is unclear. As Professor Cunliffe points out, there seems to have been a formula for making curses. Get the wording wrong and the curse could be worthless. Worse still, it might rebound on you. Domestic items have also been found. Leather sandals have been uncovered, and beautifully carved gemstones, probably used in rings. Many of the citizens of Aquae Sulis, and visitors to the city, seem to have been wealthy, and there were service industries to supply them with goods.

Other archaeological investigations have unearthed villas, workshops and market places. What is more, it is now being

suggested that Aquae Sulis was far bigger than previously thought – perhaps as big as the modern city. However, during the fourth century the city seems to have declined. There were several reasons for this. A period of localized climate warming brought higher sea and river levels, and the baths began to flood, putting them out of action at various times. Christianity, long an illicit and secret religion, in AD 312 became the official faith of the Roman Empire. The pagan symbols of the temple were thrown over, the carved stones turned face down and used for paving. The precarious situation in Rome itself meant that interest in far-flung outposts of the Empire waned. As life became more dangerous, a wall was built on top of the rampart. Slowly people withdrew within its shelter. New houses encroached on the temple precinct while the temple itself, raised four centuries before from the marsh, became a dramatic ruin.

'Wondrous is this masonry, shattered by the fates . . . the buildings raised by giants are crumbling.' These dramatic words come from an account we have of Aquae Sulis written in a poem called *The Wanderer*, probably dating from the late seventh or early eighth century. This is a Saxon voice speaking. In the two hundred years since Britain was abandoned by Rome, the Anglo-Saxons had finally taken control of the country, and the southern part of the island was now known as England and Aquae Sulis as Bathon – or sometimes as Hat Bathu (Hot Bath) or Akemancester (sometimes said to mean the town of sick people but almost certainly from Aquaemann, meaning the place of the waters). All this indicates that, despite the gloomy picture

painted by the Saxon account, the baths still functioned, although the Romans would have been dismayed at their condition. The western range seems the most likely to have survived. They were only hidden when the King's Bath was built on top, some two hundred years later. It is possible that the principal baths were used by the monks as a baptistery. Even less is known about the fate of what later became the Hot Bath and the Cross Bath, but the discovery that a lane linked the two makes it likely they were also used by the Saxons. In place of the temple there was 'a convent of holy virgins', the land for it given in AD 675 by King Osric of Mercia. By AD 757 King Offa ruled the area, the nuns had been replaced by monks and it is possible that Offa had ordered the building of the Saxon abbey. We cannot be certain where this stood but it was certainly in the vicinity of the present church.

For Bath, on the borders of the two kingdoms of Mercia and Wessex, the Saxon period was often troubled, and made more so by the Viking attacks on the country. For a time, under Alfred, the Vikings were driven off, and during this period the city wall was strengthened and a measure of rebuilding went on. Within the wall, the city streets began to assume the plan we see today, although road changes to ease traffic congestion persist throughout the centuries, right up to the present. The abbey, almost certainly constructed from blocks of stone taken from the temple ruins, was described as being of *mira fabrica* – wondrous workmanship. Perhaps because of this, together with the city's politically sensitive position, it was in Bath Abbey that the first King of all

England, Edgar, was crowned in AD 973 by Dunstan, the Archbishop of Canterbury.

This period of peace was a brief respite. The Vikings returned, and in the early years of the eleventh century the country fell to Cnut, Wessex being the last area to yield. Cnut reconciled Saxon and Dane, and brought to the country a welcome period of stability. Apart from increased taxes, for most people life went on much as before. Indeed, Bath, and the Abbey in particular, prospered under the Danish kings and their successors. Visitors came to the baths, which were administered and remodelled by the monks, country people came to the markets, and parish churches were built for the spiritual welfare of the inhabitants. Then, in 1066, William of Normandy seized the throne.

At first little changed. Although Bath was part of the King's estate, it was made over to Edith, Edward the Confessor's widow, reverting to the King on her death. For a time the Saxon monks remained undisturbed at the Abbey, and it was a Saxon abbot, Aelfsig, who rebuilt the Hot Bath in the late eleventh century and who may have constructed the lane which ran westward from the Abbey's baths to the Hot and the Cross Baths. Known later as White Hart Lane,

it would survive until it was rebuilt in the late eighteenth century, when it became Bath Street.

But in 1087 William died, to be succeeded by his son William Rufus. William II was never a popular king, and almost immediately, in 1088, there was an uprising against him. Bath suffered badly at the hands of the rebels and the Abbey itself was left almost ruined.

When William regained control, he handed the city over to his physician, a French Benedictine monk known to us as John of Tours. Appointed Bishop of Wells, John quickly moved the seat of the diocese to Bath. He tore down what was left of the Saxon abbey and built a vast new cathedral in the Romanesque style, together with a palace for himself. The Benedictines were great builders of enormous churches. The abbey at Cluny, in Burgundy, with a total length of nearly two hundred metres, was the largest in Christendom when it was built, and while the church at Bath was only about half its size, there are enough traces left to suggest that there were striking similarities between the two.

The holdings of the monastery were extended and a quarter of Bath, as well as other properties outside the city walls, was transferred to Church hands. It was John of Tours

RIGHT The setting sun picks out the silhouette of Bath Abbey, with the massive late-Victorian Empire Hotel looming on the right.

who ordered the building, over the Roman reservoir, of a new bath which soon became known as the King's Bath. Almost certainly it was linked to the infirmary.

It seems likely, too, that the French monks brought the latest technology in weaving woollen cloth, for Bath's fortunes turned away from the baths and it became a wool town. Chaucer's feisty Wife of Bath, having outlived five husbands, was rich because of the weaving trade, and independent thanks to her widowhood. Chaucer makes almost no mention of the baths, although we know they were used, and used quite riotously, for in 1449 Bishop Beckington issued an injunction to Bath to stop certain malpractices. 'When any persons, whether male or female, go to the said waters to bathe and recover their health, and through modesty and shame try to cover their privy parts, the men with drawers and the women with smocks, they, the said people [of Bath] by what they say is an established custom of the city, barbarously and shamelessly strip them of their said garments and reveal them to the gaze of the bystanders, and inflict on them not only the loss of their garments but a heavy monetary fine.' The good bishop was not prepared to tolerate this sort of behaviour and

threatened the entire city with excommunication if it did not stop. Some changes were made. Bathers over the age of puberty were not allowed to go unclothed into the water. Attempts were made to separate the sexes, but it was not until 1590 that a bath was built solely for female use, the Women's or Queen's Bath. The other baths continued to be shared. It was only in the nineteenth century, with its greater concern for propriety, that single-sex bathing once again became normal.

The city was now divided into two parts: the monastery, which administered the springs and cared for people's souls, and the city itself, now a busy market and wool town. The pattern of life in the city was set for the Middle Ages. Bath avoided the worst effects of the Wars of the Roses and became prosperous. Homes became grander and more sophisticated, a bridge was built replacing the ford at the river crossing south of the city, and water supplies were piped into the city from cold-water springs in the surrounding hillsides. Permanent shops, rather than simple stalls, were built in the marketplace. One of these early shops still survives at 21 High Street. There may well be others hidden away behind Georgian façades.

RIGHT The west door of Bath Abbey is flanked by its patron saints, Peter and Paul. Peter (to the left) has lost his halo and part of his head, probably as a consequence of damage during the Civil War. A new face was carved out of his beard.

FAR LEFT, TOP Light catches on the massive windows of the Abbey. It is said that four-sevenths of the surface area of the building is glass.

FAR LEFT, BOTTOM The rebus of Bishop Oliver King – a punning picture in which his name is represented by a bishop's mitre, an olive tree, and a king's crown.

LEFT Angels climb up and down the ladder. The one coming down head first is bringing the word of God back to earth. On either side are figures of disciples and a female figure, thought to be the Virgin Mary.

RIGHT The west front of Bath Abbey, showing the dream of Oliver King. Above the great west window a heavenly host looks up at Christ riding in glory.

The one building that failed to flourish was the Abbey itself. In fact it was no longer strictly a cathedral, for the bishops had increasingly shown a preference for Wells. It was now officially a priory, and as such did not receive the subsidies that were needed to care for the fabric of the building. By 1499, when the new Bishop of Bath and Wells arrived to view his church, it was in poor condition. This bishop's name was Oliver King, and he was secretary to Henry VII, the victor in the Wars of the Roses. Undoubtedly he was appointed because he was a man on whom Henry Tudor could rely. Having seized the throne from Richard III, Henry had no intention of letting it go. The West Country was always going to be a likely place for other claimants to start an insurrection, and trustworthy Bishop King would be on hand to give Henry an early warning of trouble.

When Oliver King arrived in Bath he was dismayed not only at the state of the church, but also by the behaviour of the monks, whom he accused of feasting and entertaining women. He decided to start his reforms by rebuilding the church. Not only would this be a pious act, but it would also have political overtones – a new start under a new dynasty. If there was any opposition to this plan, King was able to win over the doubters by telling of a strange vision that had come to him in a dream while he was staying in Bath. He had seen, he said, a host of angels worshipping the Holy Trinity, while other angels ascended and descended a ladder leading from heaven to earth. Then a voice spoke to Oliver and proclaimed, 'Let an olive establish the crown and a king restore the church!' Since he, Oliver, was helping to establish the crown, then clearly he, King, was being commanded by God to restore the church. Whether God indulges in heavy-handed punning is questionable, but it convinced the locals.

Conveniently for Oliver King, the previous prior had just died, so a new prior supportive of King's plans, William Bird, could be elected. Henry VII himself took considerable interest in the project, and his own stonemasons, the Vertue brothers, provided the designs. Work started at a tremendous pace and the modern visitor can still admire much of that five-hundred-year-old craftsmanship. The great clerestory windows were state-of-the-art technology in 1500, and on a sunny day, when light pours into the nave, it is easy to see why the church is called the Lantern of the West. Oliver King's dream was carved on the west front, and on each side of it there was carved an olive tree, encircled by a crown and surmounted by a bishop's mitre. This rebus, or punning

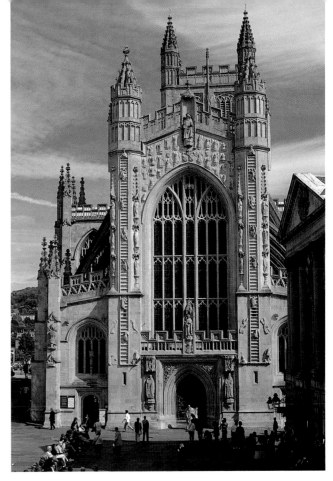

design, reminds viewers of the church's founder. Meanwhile, the church's patron saints, Peter and Paul, were placed on either side of the west door.

The east front went up so quickly that it was complete before the plans were finalized. The square-headed east window and other structural details all indicate that the first idea was to have a flat roof in the chancel but, as work pressed ahead, the Vertue brothers changed their minds and introduced fan vaulting. The speedy construction was possible because great chunks of the Norman cathedral were used as foundations and walls. Some of them can still be seen today. Through a grille in the floor the visitor can look down on the bases of the Norman pillars, which were used as the footings for the Tudor ones, while a Norman arch is clearly visible, turned into a window, in the chapel in the south-east corner. Part of the tower remains at the eastern end, its stairway utilized by the Tudor builders to give access to the roof. On the outside, the bases of other pillars are visible at the east end of the church, while in the north-east corner an arch can still be seen bricked into the wall. This arch, and a matching one on the other side, remained until the seventeenth century, when the east end was tidied up and a doorway inserted. The arches can be seen on early-seventeenth-century maps, such as Savile's map of around 1600. (These maps are more like bird's-eye views of the city than true plans and show a variety of sometimes intriguing

ABOVE The Abbey seen from the south-east.

PAGES 30–31 Bath Abbey, interior view, showing part of the south transept and the south aisle of the nave. The lamp, intended originally for gas light, was made to a nineteenth-century design based on a fifteenth-century Norwegian original.

detail.) When we consider that the present church occupies only the nave of John of Tours' cathedral, it gives some idea of the size of the Norman church.

Rapid though the work was, it was not fast enough for the changing political and religious circumstances. Henry VII died in 1509. Work continued under Prior Bird, who constructed a chantry chapel in the Abbey, where carved birds hidden among the foliage preserve his name for posterity. However, when a restoration of the Abbey was carried out in 1833 it was noticed that the chapel was not complete. Portions remained ready for the carver but the work had not been carried out. The fan vaulting was completed only in the chancel – what we now see in the nave is Victorian. It was certainly intended to be there. Turner's watercolour of Bath Abbey, painted in 1796, clearly shows odd pieces of stonework projecting from the side walls of the Abbey just below the parapet. They are also shown, though rather less clearly, on Savile's map. They are the tops of what were intended to be flying buttresses, an absolute requirement of fan vaulting, which exercises an outward thrust on the walls. Why did work suddenly come to a halt when the church was so nearly complete? The answer lies with the matrimonial arrangements of Henry VIII.

Henry VIII was the last Roman Catholic king of England. Until the Act of Supremacy of 1534, though the

King held temporal power, spiritual power lay with the Pope. Bath Abbey still bears the relics of that Catholic past, with the symbols of Christ's Passion carved in the spandrels of the great west door, and a cardinal's hat over a coat of arms in the chancel (this belonged to an absentee Bishop of Bath and Wells, Adriano di Castello). But when the Pope refused to annul Henry's marriage to Katharine of Aragon (who had not provided him with the longed-for male heir) so that he could marry Anne Boleyn, Henry broke with Rome, founded the Church of England, and took over all Church properties. Being short of money, he then proceeded to sell off the monasteries, many of which were hugely rich.

The King's commissioners arrived in Bath in 1535, and reported back to Thomas Cromwell, Henry's minister, that the prior, one Gibbs, was 'a right virtuous man' though 'simple and not of the greatest wit'. The monks, however, were accused of having sexual relations with men and women. Modern commentators have pointed out that the commissioners were biased, and of course they were looking for reasons to close monasteries, but in fairness to them it should be noted that their report has similarities with Oliver King's account of forty years before. Gibbs desperately tried to fend off the inevitable, even offering Cromwell a pension. All his efforts were futile. The priory closed in 1539 and the monks and prior were pensioned off. The church was

ABOVE LEFT The walls are
lined with monuments, some of
visitors who left it too late to
take the waters. Immediately
beneath the window in the
foreground is the plaque to
Sir Isaac Pitman, inventor of
Pitman's shorthand.

ABOVE RIGHT Most of the
Abbey's stained glass, including
this injunction to watch and pray,
is Victorian.

offered to the city for the sum of 500 marks. This was apparently a fair offer; nevertheless, the city turned it down. They had good reason. The King was in the habit of selling off lands cheaply and then accusing the purchasers of cheating him, with predictably unpleasant results. The City Council of Bath had no intention of being caught like that.

So the windows were stripped of their glass, the roof of its lead, the bells taken down, and all were sold, along with any removable ironwork. The great church became a shell. The entire property, including lands at Bathwick, Smallcombe, Holloway, Lyncombe and Widcombe, was first sold to Humphrey Colles. He then sold on the city properties to the Colthurst family, who turned the prior's lodging into a private house and the cloister garden into a Tudor knot garden. The land south of the abbey remained in the family's hands until 1612.

The Colthursts, however, had no use for a ruined church, and in 1572 they presented it to the city. Almost certainly the city did not want it. The inhabitants had churches of their own; they had no need of the monastery's church, now urgently in want of repair. Not only that, but, astonishingly, bits and pieces of the Norman church were still standing around on the east side, 'laid to waste and unroofed', according to John Leland. However, the Council immediately began to make good use of the land on the

north side of the church by erecting houses along the north wall – thus reducing the cost of their construction. These buildings, which included shops, bake-houses and even a couple of pubs, were finally demolished in the mid-nineteenth century; roof marks can still be detected here and there on the Abbey walls.

Then a scheme was put forward to consolidate the city within the walls into one great parish, with a refurbished Abbey at its centre. A petition was sent to Queen Elizabeth to ask if money could be raised nationally for the project. It is a matter for conjecture to what extent this sprang from a genuine desire to restore the once magnificent building, and how much it came from a wish to please the Queen: the church had been promoted by her grandfather. Alternatively, the City Fathers may have considered that a grand parish church would impress visitors and hence be good for tourism. In any event, the plea was successful. In 1574 Elizabeth herself visited Bath, presumably to keep an eye on the work in progress. By 1576, the date carved on the exterior of the south transept, the chancel and transepts were usable. It is said that it was Elizabeth who decreed that the church should be known by its old name of Bath Abbey, even though it was now just a parish church, dedicated to St Peter and St Paul. In 1590 she granted the city a charter, which meant that the Council officially became Bath Corporation.

LEFT The chancel of Bath Abbey. The fan vaulting is the original sixteenth-century design by the Vertue brothers. The stained glass window is a particularly fine example of the work of the Victorian glaziers Clayton and Bell.

RIGHT The vaulting in the nave was put in place by George Gilbert Scott during his restoration of 1868. It replaced a lath and plaster roof constructed on the orders of Bishop James Montagu.

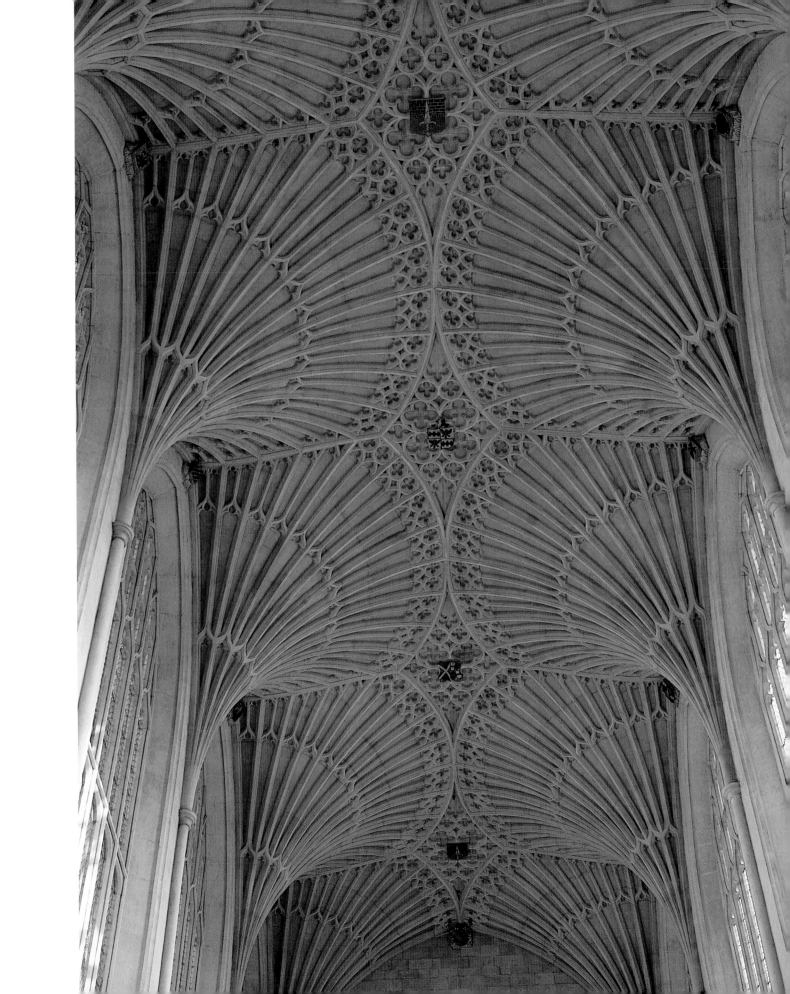

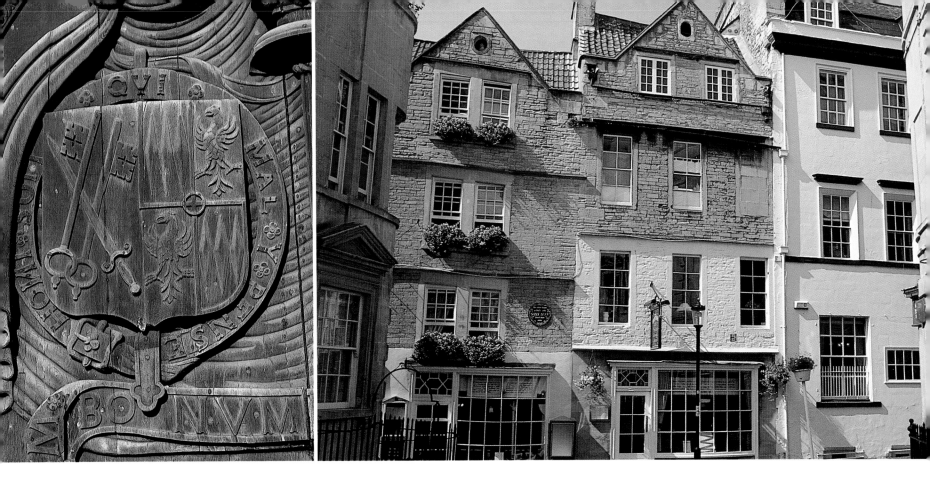

ABOVE LEFT Detail from the Abbey doors, showing Bishop Montagu's coat of arms. On the left side is the coat of arms of Winchester, where Montagu became bishop after his tenure as Bishop of Bath and Wells. On the right are the arms of the Montagu family.

ABOVE RIGHT Sally Lunn's House and the old Star and Garter pub, now part of the Huntsman, seen from Gallaway's Buildings. Before the Georgian builders began work much of Bath must have looked like this.

Despite Elizabeth's apparent approval of the refurbishment done in her name, work was slow and much of the nave remained in poor condition. After her death her godson Sir John Harington, who lived locally, seems to have kept his eye on what was happening, and to have been unimpressed with what he saw. A rather charming local legend tells us that in 1608 the new bishop, James Montagu, was walking in town with Sir John when it began to rain heavily. Sir John, who was famous for his jokes, invited the Bishop to shelter in the church, where he found, as Harington well knew, that it was raining as hard inside as out. 'If the church does not keep us safe from the water above, how shall it save others from the fire below?' inquired Sir John. The Bishop took the hint and put building in hand, in particular reroofing the nave. His family also contributed generously to the work. The great oak doors at the west end were given by his brother Henry. Restored in 2003, they look set to face another four hundred years of British weather.

Additions, alterations and renovations went on during the ensuing centuries, notably in the nineteenth century when no less than three restorations took place, some more historically accurate than others. The organ screen, which separated the nave from the choir, was removed, and the pews installed. Although they are based on a medieval design, they dominate the church, and it has lost the sense of spaciousness it must once have had, a quality remarked upon in the seventeenth century by Thomas Fuller, who said, 'This church is both spacious and specious, most lightsome as ever I beheld, proceeding from the greatness of the windows and the whiteness of the glass therein.' Despite the addition of Victorian stained glass windows his comments about the lightness still hold true today.

It was during Elizabeth's reign that tourism began to expand. With the wool trade in recession, the Corporation needed to find a new source of income. The political and religious situation came to the rescue. Elizabeth and her ministers became concerned about the use of holy wells. As they were associated with Roman Catholic saints, visits to them were suppressed, but high-ranking English Catholics used this as an excuse to visit foreign spas, in particular the most famous of them, Spa, from which all derived their generic name. Here they gathered in great numbers and, the Government suspected, plotted with Catholics from Spain, Spa being under Spanish control. It was decided to encourage visits to English watering places for medicinal reasons. All the baths underwent extensive remodelling and a small bath for the poor sick was added to the Hot Bath in about 1576. Known as the Lepers' Bath, it was tiny – a mere four metres square.

ABOVE Abbey Green. In Norman times this area was part of the cathedral close. The Crystal Palace, which has been a pub since 1851, stands on a Roman property. A tessellated floor was discovered beneath its cellars.

Elizabeth helped to set the fashion by her visit to Bath in 1574. Nevertheless, spas, even Bath, were to retain an aura of 'Popery' until all religious associations were swept away in the social whirl of the eighteenth century. This was probably in part a consequence of the Stuart enthusiasm for spas. It is interesting that among the apparently innocent visitors in August 1605 were members of the dissident group later to be responsible for the Gunpowder Plot.

Rather ironically, however, the first Stuart to manifest an interest in spas was the wife of the staunchly Protestant James I. Anne of Denmark came to Bath for her health and was so pleased with the efficacy of the waters that she repeated the experience. It was during James's reign that building licences were granted for the old monastery land which later became known as Abbey Green. This included the present Sally Lunn's House and an alehouse called the Raven, now a fish and chip shop. (Though Sally Lunn's House defiantly declares itself to be over six hundred years old, the building can be no earlier than 1622, when building leases for this part of the town were first granted.) Some of the houses on Abbey Green were refronted in the eighteenth century but during renovation work at 3 Abbey Green, old timbering and lath and plaster walls were discovered. Seventeenth-century mullioned windows are still visible at the sides of these apparently Georgian buildings.

However, in 1625 Charles I came to the throne. His confrontations with Parliament and suspicions that he planned to return England to the Catholic fold caused unrest and divisions, even within families. From 1642 the structure of society was shaken by the cataclysmic events of the Civil War. At first Bath, like the rest of Somerset, supported the King, but the city had a history of Puritanism. Eventually the city declared itself for Parliament, although the decision was not unanimous. The authorities were constantly worried about Cavalier plotters trying to win over the disaffected. Bath remained an important symbolic prize, although strategically it can have been of little significance. The first battle in the immediate area was on the hills of Lansdown in 1643, a skirmish that both sides claimed as a victory. The Parliamentarians continued to hold Bath. However, fortunes were reversed just days later when Waller's forces, in pursuit of the Royalist army, were roundly defeated at Devizes. Bath fell into Royalist hands, a situation that pleased many shopkeepers and innholders. Royal visitors, including the King and the Prince of Wales, came in considerable numbers. If Royalist prisoners could establish a medical reason to visit spas, they were sometimes given temporary leave of absence from their place of confinement to do so – on payment of substantial bonds. During 1644, the King appealed to the Parliamentarians to allow his friend and faithful supporter Sir Gervase Scroope to visit Bath for his health. In this instance Scroope's son was prepared to be held prisoner in his father's stead.

By 1646 the Parliamentary party was in control. Fashionable society was, as always, welcome to Bath. Rather less welcome were the war-wounded sent by Parliament. Admittedly Parliament donated some money towards funding them but in 1653, when yet another batch of wounded soldiers was about to make a visit, the Corporation took a stand. They said that the city was 'much impoverished' and refused point-blank to give any money to 'any lame or maimed soldiers or others'. The presence of recuperating military men might have been good for Bath's reputation as a centre of healing, but it did little to promote the city as a fashionable resort. During this time the city seems to have become rather shabby. The diarist John Evelyn, coming in 1654, described the streets as 'uneven, narrow, and unpleasant'. Particularly notorious were Westgate Street, Stall Street and Cheap Street, where the buildings were packed in, and overhung the roadway.

It is perhaps hardly surprising to learn that on the restoration of Charles II in 1660, Bath was the first city to proclaim the new king. Many of Parliament's original supporters were thoroughly disillusioned by Cromwell, and had actively campaigned for Charles's return. The city was rewarded in 1668 by a visit from the King. Among the royal entourage was Samuel Pepys, who presents a picture of Bath very different from Evelyn's. He says the town was 'most of stone, and clean, though the streets generally narrow' and admired the 'very fair stone houses'. One of the houses which Pepys may have admired still stands in the Sawclose; it is now a bar. The stone, although a local limestone, is not the honey-coloured Bath stone, but a pale grey lias stone.

Not all Pepys's impressions were favourable. He dismissed the preacher in the Abbey as a vain pragmatic fellow and fell asleep during one of his sermons. On his visit to the Cross Bath, he commented: 'Methinks it cannot be clean to go so many bodies together in the same water.' He noticed too that, although this was the coolest bath, the springs were in some parts so hot 'as the feet [are] not able

RIGHT High on Lansdown stands a monument to one of the Royalist generals, Sir Bevil Granville (or Grenville), who was mortally wounded in a skirmish on the hilltop during the Civil War.

to endure'. By and large, however, it seems to have been a happy visit, with good company and good conversation.

Despite Pepys's enthusiasm, the indications were that not all was well. There were complaints about the state of lodgings and little was offered in the way of sophisticated entertainment. Immediately east of the Abbey were the gravel walks later to be known as the Grove (and, after a visit by Prince William of Orange in 1734, as Orange Grove), laid out in the French style of straight rows of trees with gravel beneath, but this was one of the few concessions to fashionable pursuits. The city seemed rather complacent. After all, royal visits still continued. Mary of Modena, wife of James II, came in an attempt to cure her infertility, and later, when William and Mary came to the throne, Mary's sister Princess Anne was another visitor. Her first visit seemed inauspicious for, having given Anne a good time, the City Fathers were reprimanded by Mary. The two sisters loathed each other, and the Queen saw the jollities laid on for Anne as a personal slight. As long as Mary was on the throne Anne's subsequent visits had to be subdued affairs. However, Anne understood the difficulty and returned to the city as Queen. The year was 1702. The city was still crammed within the walls and the lodging-houses now looked unfashionable and dirty. Yet, persuaded by the monarch's affection for Bath, the aristocracy was beginning

to descend on the city in increasing numbers. Changes would have to be made if Bath were to capitalize on this opportunity. Other spas, although lacking the benefit of hot waters, were anxious to assume the mantle of top spa. Fortunately for Bath, entrepreneurs of all kinds were eager to seize their chance, and it was their enterprise and business acumen that created the city that we enjoy today.

Among the most successful were three vigorous and very different men who were all determined, each in his own way, to transform Bath. One was a Welshman who, having failed as undergraduate, soldier and law student, had turned gambler to earn a living. In 1705 he came to Bath, as did other gamblers, invalids, fortune-hunters and gentry. He seems an unlikely hero, yet he had a deep love of order that was to transform Bath. He was accustomed to mingle with fashionable society and he saw that much was lacking. At first there was little he could do. In charge of all social events was a Master of Ceremonies, appointed by the Duke of Beaufort. In 1705 this was a rough local gambler called Webster who was quite content with procedures in the town, since they fitted well with his own behaviour. Surprisingly, the two gamblers became friends, and Webster appointed the stranger his deputy. Before long, Webster's dissolute lifestyle was his downfall. Challenged to that occupational hazard of gamblers, a duel, he lost his life in the Grove

ABOVE LEFT An approximate translation of the Greek inscription in the pediment of the Pump Room is 'Water is Best' – an appropriate motto for the city.

ABOVE RIGHT At night, onlookers in the Abbey Church Yard can gaze into the lit interior of the Pump Room.

where he was accustomed to strut as Master of Ceremonies. On this occasion the Corporation appears to have acted promptly and wisely. The deputy became the new Master, and thus in 1705 began the reign of the most famous Master of Ceremonies of them all, Richard 'Beau' Nash. In the Victorian age writers frequently disapproved of Nash, and even today there are those who feel that his importance is overstated. Yet comments from his contemporaries in Bath make clear his influence on the city. He saw that without the refinements to which fashionable society was accustomed in London, Bath could not compete as a social centre.

The Corporation had already noticed the increased enthusiasm for drinking the waters rather than just bathing, and in 1704–6 a Pump Room was built, to a light and airy design by John Harvey. Almost immediately there was criticism that it was too small and had an insufficient supply of water for the crowds who flocked there. We know what it looked like, from a picture on a corridor in the present Pump Room. We see no tables or chairs, but people chatting, dancing, flirting, while water is dispensed and the musicians play. 'The Musick', as it was known in the eighteenth century, was introduced by Nash. A doctor who was sceptical about Bath's claim to healing powers threatened to put a toad in the spring to deter people from using it. Nash brought down from London musicians who, he said, would charm the creature from the waters. It seems to have been a good excuse to improve the quality of musicianship in the Pump Room.

In 1751 the Pump Room was extended but by 1786 Thomas Baldwin was working on plans for a new room. Unfortunately, his inability to render his accounts resulted in his dismissal before the project was complete, and John Palmer was brought in to finish the work. It has often been said that the interior is by Palmer and that Baldwin, although producing delightful work on the west side, lost his inspiration on the rather weak north side. However, in 1998 some lost plans by both Baldwin and Palmer turned up. These revealed the truth. The interior is a reduced version of Baldwin's original plans, and it was Palmer who was responsible for the inferior north façade.

Some features were retained from the old Pump Room. Thomas Tompion, the great London clockmaker, had given two timepieces to the Pump Room: a sundial to tell the time for bathers in the King's Bath, and a magnificent longcase clock for the room itself. Both can still be seen today, as can the statue of Beau Nash with his hand resting on a plinth from which hang the plans for the General Hospital, his favourite charity. The design of the room includes a reference to the Roman discoveries that were made while it was being planned, for the columns are a copy of those on the temple of Minerva which lies beneath.

ABOVE The Pump Room was the place for visitors to drink their regular glass of water, dance a little to the music and chatter to their friends. Today, tea and coffee are more popular refreshments.

In 1708 Nash persuaded Thomas Harrison to build the first Assembly Rooms. Now there was also somewhere to gather to drink tea and coffee, and play at cards. Although another set of rooms was built close by in 1727, and a third opened to the north of the city in 1771, Harrison's remained the principal rooms until they burnt down in 1820.

Nash's outstanding achievement was to impose order on a society that, for a variety of reasons, had no wish to accept it. He laid down rules of behaviour, particularly for attendance at balls, which, though facetiously expressed, encapsulated a measure of good sense. For example, one rule stated that all whisperers of lies and scandal be taken to be their authors; this was a brave attempt to stop trouble-making in this city where gossip was one of the pleasures of society. More seriously, he sought to curb the practice of duelling. It was clearly unacceptable, in a place where gambling made arguments likely, to condone the settling of arguments by resorting to sword and pistol; moreover, he can have had no desire to go the same way as his predecessor. He also set out a timetable, so that at almost any time of day visitors knew what they should be doing, and, as we have seen, he introduced a better class of musicians into the Pump Room. If what he created was not exactly a theme park, it could certainly be described as an artificial playground where amusements were carefully organized and controlled.

The second man responsible for the profound change in Bath was, like Nash, not native to the city. He was a young Cornishman, Ralph Allen, appointed postmaster in 1712 at the startlingly early age of nineteen. The postal service at this time was expensive, inefficient and open to corruption. The system worked if everyone did their job properly, but no one ever did. Moreover, post was meant to travel up and down set post roads. Two towns quite close to each other might find themselves on different post roads, which meant that letters sent between them had to travel to London and back again. As postage was calculated by mileage, this was not only slow, but expensive. Country postmasters such as Allen would pay the Government for the right to run a 'farm' of postal services, and some introduced cross-posts. The tricky part for a postmaster was to avoid corruption among the people working for him. Allen took on a huge 'farm' stretching from Oxford down to Exeter and up to Chester. For this he had to pay the exchequer £6000 per annum — more than £500,000 in modern terms. Such was Allen's business acumen that he became a rich man, able to invest in other developments such as the local stone quarries. Not unnaturally, he was keen to see a market for the stone, and in this capacity he acted as patron to the third member of our triumvirate, Bath-born architect John Wood. We will hear more of Wood in the next chapter. Here we should note

LEFT The King's Bath. With the water lowered, we can see the steps, known as slips, down which eighteenth-century invalids would descend into the waters. Above is the Pump Room.

RIGHT, TOP The entrance to the Pump Room.

RIGHT, BOTTOM Part of the colonnaded screen wall on the west side of the Pump Room.

ABOVE LEFT Richard 'Beau' Nash stands proudly in his niche in the Pump Room, his hand resting on a column on which are displayed the plans for the General Hospital. The statue is by the Bath sculptor Prince Hoare.

ABOVE RIGHT The portrait of Ralph Allen by his friend the artist William Hoare, Prince Hoare's elder brother. It hangs in the banqueting room of the Guildhall.

that, in addition to his architectural achievements, he was the author of *An Essay Towards a Description of Bath*, first published in 1742, with a revised edition in 1749 and a posthumous edition in 1765. This is a work from which much of our knowledge of Bath in the first half of the eighteenth century is derived.

Allen was fortunate in his choice of friends. He also had a talent for being in the right place at the right time. When Queen Anne died in 1714 and George I became king, there was a fear that the West Country would declare for the Stuart James III. In Bristol there were pro-Stuart riots on Coronation Day. General Wade was sent down to keep order, and the young Bath postmaster was able to supply him with intelligence about Jacobite plans. Undoubtedly Allen made this discovery by opening mail of which he was suspicious, but we should not read into his actions anything sinister or underhand. The Government granted warrants for deputies to open suspect mail. Wade subsequently befriended the young man. All of this did Allen's standing in the city no harm at all, especially when, in 1722, Wade became Member of Parliament for Bath. By 1725, Allen himself was a freeman of the city and he was elected councillor later in the year. He became so influential that although he served only one year as mayor, in 1742, it was generally agreed that he controlled the city during the entire

time of his service on the Council. A scurrilous cartoon, published in 1763, portrayed the Council as the 'One-headed Corporation', Ralph Allen's being the single head.

Nash and Allen could not be described as friends. They moved in different circles, the former in the butterfly world of fashionable society, the latter in the respectable world of clergy and Corporation. However, in the eighteenth century these worlds were by no means mutually exclusive: the two had shared acquaintances and certainly met on occasion. For example, Nash, Allen and Wood were all involved in the establishment of the Mineral Water Hospital (see page 70). Both Allen and Nash could be relied upon to help with charitable works. Indeed, when Nash was old and destitute and in need of charity himself, Allen helped him out, despite his probable antipathy for Nash's way of life. Their portraits give away the differences. In Nash, we see a bold, dissipated rakish figure, while Ralph Allen stares out, ascetic, calm, dressed in sober clothes. The eyes, however, are curiously similar, challenging and determined. Neither, one feels, would have been a good man to cross.

Nash and Allen were not, however, the only opportunists to leap on the bandwagon. Some members of the Corporation were also developers and architects, while others were shopkeepers, brewers, bankers, apothecaries and innkeepers. Even today, Bath is not short of pubs; in the seventeenth and eighteenth centuries, streets such as Cheap Street were lined with drinking places of all types, from simple beerhouses to inns of the highest quality. For centuries the largest was the Bear, which looked down Stall Street and in future years was to cause problems for people coming from the new parts of town to the baths. Trembling invalids were carried through its noisy stable yard, with coaches constantly coming and going, horses being led to and fro, and even an undertaker's workshop in one corner – not the ideal sight for Bath's valetudinarian visitors. Eventually, in 1806, it was torn down and Union Street built in its place, linking the upper town and the city centre. Like many of the other inns, the Bear was Corporation property. Members of the Corporation, or their families or reliable friends or servants, ran many of these inns. It was clearly in their interests to keep the tourists coming, and they were well placed to do so.

Bath Corporation was enormously powerful. There were no free elections. Existing councillors elected new councillors from the Freemen, a body which they themselves controlled and selected. They also selected Bath's two Members of Parliament, and administered justice through-out the city. Anyone researching Bath's history finds the same names cropping up again and again. Families such as the Chapmans, the Atwoods, the Collibees and, of course, the Allens recur in document after document.

Yet for all this power, the first Guildhall was a rather obscure building, away behind the market area. In 1590 it was moved to the centre of the Market Place (the present High Street), although it seems to have been more of a market hall than a true guildhall, standing on pillars with market stalls beneath the council chamber. In 1625 it was rebuilt, although very much on the same plan. The rooms were also used for balls and entertaining. Despite various refurbishments, this arrangement was still not ideal for a town with claims to elegance. Discussions about a new building, more worthy of the Corporation, began in 1760, but every time an architect presented a plan it was successfully opposed by one of the councillors on the building committee, Thomas Warr Atwood. It comes as no surprise to find that he himself was a builder with pretensions to being an architect. It comes as even less of a surprise to learn that in 1775 he finally secured the contract for the work, despite a last-ditch attempt by two other architects to persuade the Corporation to opt for something better.

Fate, however, took a hand. Atwood was inspecting an old building when the floor gave way and he fell through. The accident was to prove fatal. His clerk, Thomas Baldwin, was then appointed to take on the design and construction of a new Guildhall, and it is his work that now dominates the High Street.

RIGHT A seagull contemplates
the dome on the Guildhall. The
dome was not part of Baldwin's
design, but was added when the
late Victorian extensions were built.

Baldwin's Guildhall brought a new elegance to the affairs of Bath Corporation; at last they had a meeting place fit for the expanding city – though, strangely, no room was set aside purely as a council chamber. While there was every facility for feeding, refreshing and otherwise entertaining the councillors and their friends, it was a room designed to be a drawing room which was used as the council room. The finest room in the Guildhall, indeed probably the finest room in Bath, is the banqueting room. Here Baldwin, influenced by the latest ideas of Robert Adam, produced what Walter Ison rightly calls 'a masterpiece of late-eighteenth-century decoration'. All the motifs that are associated with neoclassical architecture are here – rams' heads, honeysuckle, garlands of husks arranged in a glory of green and gold.

Here, too, are portraits of the great and good: George III and his wife Charlotte, his father Frederick, Prince of Wales, and his autocratic wife Augusta, as well as some of the aristocracy with connections in the city. Pride of place, however, is reserved for a small portrait of a soberly dressed businessman: Ralph Allen (see page 44).

Trials were also held in the Guildhall. This is the reason for the figure of Justice standing on top of the Guildhall, holding scales and a sword. It is often pointed out that she is not blindfold, but this is not as rare as people often think. What is unusual is that the statue is probably based on a portrait by its sculptor, Robert Edge Pine, of the eighteenth-century historian Catherine Macaulay. She was famous for her strong republican views, and her writings influenced the men behind the American Revolution.

Two flanking wings were built in 1893, in a florid Baroque style, by a young Scottish architect, John McKean Brydon. The northern wing housed the Technical School while the southern wing contained new municipal offices. Illustrative friezes on each corner indicate the building's original purposes. Classical figures hold suitable symbols, and while this works for the municipal offices, it is a trifle incongruous to see Roman ladies and gentlemen clutching examples of Victorian engineering. The Victoria Art Gallery was added six years later, to house Bath's collection of paintings, sculpture and decorative arts.

However, all this was still far in the future when Richard Nash and Ralph Allen were young and the stage was being set for the expansion which was to attract society from Europe, as well as all over the British Isles. Despite the changes of the early eighteenth century, for many years there

LEFT The northern Guildhall extension, designed by the Scottish architect John McKean Brydon, was the Technical School, and the figures in the frieze carry accessories to suggest subjects taught there.

RIGHT, TOP The figure of Justice, here providing a vantage point for a disrespectful seagull. Designed by Robert Edge Pine, it is said to have been based on the historian and republican Catherine Macaulay.

RIGHT, BOTTOM At the far end of Bath Street is this little house, built around 1800 as the Museum of Bath's Antiquities. The statues may be from one of the city gates or the old Guildhall. It is now part of the new spa complex.

was still much to criticize when the weary traveller finally reached Bath. John Wood's 1749 description of the various baths is not encouraging. Cold winds swept across one bath, and the steps by which bathers entered were dark, cold and slippery. Gradually, over the years, the baths were improved. The Duke of Kingston had a suite of private baths built to the south of the Abbey in 1755. The excavations for the foundations exposed the Roman baths to view for the first time since the Saxon period, although still no one had any idea of the extent of the establishment. An antiquarian friend of the Duke's, Mr Lucas, made a note of the findings before the private baths were placed on top. The Duke's baths were removed in 1922 when the Roman baths were opened to the public. By 1778, John Wood's son, also John

RIGHT The south wall of the banqueting room, showing the exquisite neoclassical decoration and three of the portraits.

BELOW, TOP A detail from the decoration in the banqueting room of the Guildhall. It shows a ram's head or aegricane.

BELOW, BOTTOM A detail of one of the chandeliers by William Parker of London. They cost Bath Corporation £266 for the three – today they are priceless.

Wood, had rebuilt the Hot Bath and in 1784 Baldwin was responsible for the delightfully light reconstruction of the Cross Bath with its serpentine façade. Today, both these baths form part of the modern spa development.

Transport of goods was one of the problems Bath faced in the eighteenth century. Roads were appalling. In the mid-seventeenth century they were probably the worst they had been in the city's history. Early in the eighteenth century Bath Corporation petitioned Parliament to allow improvements along the Great Bath Road, and its turnpiking brought some relief.

However, in 1727 the River Avon had finally been made navigable from Bristol to Bath. It had taken a long battle to achieve this. Many landowners, not to mention mine-owners and colliers, were against it. It is often forgotten that Bath was in a coal-mining area, with pits just a mile or two from the city. The slag heaps were ploughed in long ago, but when the soil is newly turned in the fields where once they stood, the blackness still shows through. The Somerset coalminers greatly feared an influx of superior Shropshire coal, so much so that there was an attempt to blow up a lock at Saltford. But a consortium of interested parties, which included the Duke of Beaufort and Ralph Allen, proved irresistible. This new development meant that fresh food and desirable merchandise arriving at the port of Bristol could swiftly be on sale in Bath. It also meant that timber and other commodities necessary for building could be brought to the city.

In the same year that the river opened up, John Wood tells us that the lodging-houses had floorboards stained brown with soot and small beer to hide the dirt, that their doors were light and thin, with varnished iron locks. The furniture was inferior and the carpets cheap. Both John Wood and Ralph Allen had plans to improve the town, and Allen was anxious to use the stone from his quarries at Combe Down. Both saw the town's deficiencies as their opportunity to expand. Other developers too saw their chance. The walls were about to come down.

THE RIVER AVON

LEFT The Avon Walkway passes beside Green Park.

RIGHT, CLOCKWISE FROM TOP LEFT Old warehouses; Dredge's Suspension Bridge; a narrowboat makes its way upriver towards the canal.

PALLADIAN PALACES

THE EARLY GEORGIAN EXPANSION

PALLADIAN PALACES
THE EARLY GEORGIAN EXPANSION

Until time travel becomes a possibility, anyone wishing to gain an impression of Bath in the early eighteenth century would do best to visit one of the larger Cotswold towns, such as Cirencester, Tetbury or Chipping Campden. Even here, Georgian façades, with all their grandeur and symmetry, have been imposed on older buildings, but the architecture is mainly that of the seventeenth century. The roofs are gabled and many houses still have mullioned windows, although sash windows became so fashionable during the eighteenth century that even little cottages acquired them. There is a pleasing variety of size and shape, and here and there jettied buildings have upper floors which overhang the pavement. So must the centre of Bath have appeared about 1700. Little of it remains, however. A new style of architecture was introduced to the city and the old was gradually swept away. Based on Roman architecture, it was inspired by the work of a sixteenth-century Italian from Vicenza called Andrea di Pietro della Gondola. He is known to us as Andrea Palladio.

Palladio visited Roman sites, including Rome itself, and read books on architecture not only by experts of his own day but also by the great Roman architect Vitruvius. He assembled all his ideas about classical architecture into a work first published in 1570: *I Quattro Libri dell' Architettura* (The Four Books of Architecture). As well as documenting the basic principles of symmetry and harmonic proportion which he used in designing villas, churches and other public buildings, it also included practical advice for builders, with woodcut illustrations to explain the text.

It was Inigo Jones, Surveyor-General to the Office of Works of James I, who introduced Palladian architecture to England. Jones's heavily annotated version of *I Quattro Libri* shows how carefully he studied Palladio. His own view of architecture was that it should be 'solid, proportional according to the rules, masculine and unaffected'. Among the buildings he designed according to these principles were the Banqueting House in Whitehall and the Queen's House at Greenwich.

If Inigo Jones revered Palladio, Jones himself was the life-long hero of Bath architect John Wood. Through Jones's eyes, Wood looked back to the purity of Palladio. It must have come as a shock to him to discover that there were plenty of other builders and budding architects in Bath who were prepared to exploit the fashion for Palladian-style building without worrying too much about the thinking behind it.

John Wood's early life is obscure. Although he seems to have been of lowly birth and possibly attended the charity school in Bath, at some stage he acquired a smattering of knowledge of various Latin authors, as well as of

contemporary writers. He worked in London, and by the age of seventeen is said to have been preparing to build a house on the Cavendish estate north of Oxford Street. It was here that he made aristocratic contacts. In 1725, when he was twenty, he turned his attention to his native city, sending some ideas to Mr Gay, who owned land in London and Bath. It was another two years before he actually returned to Bath, where he found that redevelopment was already well under way. George Trim, a clothier and councillor, had developed his land just north of the city wall as early as 1707, while other entrepreneurs were casting their eyes over land to the south, between the city wall and the River Avon. As it turned out, this was not very wise, for the Ham and the Ambury, as these areas were known, were on the flood plain. The disadvantages of this soon became apparent. What started as respectable middle-class housing was eventually abandoned to landlords who filled every room with the poor who could not afford to live anywhere else.

Elsewhere in Bath local architects were also busy. John Harvey had designed the first Pump Room, and others, including Thomas Greenway, William Killigrew and John Strahan of Bristol, were equally active. Greenway had designed a Cold Bath, utilizing springs at Widcombe. A fine structure in the Palladian style, it was demolished in the 1960s. One Greenway house that remains is now a pub, the Garrick's Head, in the Sawclose. Although slightly over-elaborate, it is finely proportioned. The windows are typical of their time, with thick glazing bars and small panes arranged 'nine over nine'. The first occupant was the 'King of Bath', Beau Nash. He lived here until 1735, when he moved to a smaller house, also designed by Greenway. This is now a restaurant known as Popjoy's, after Nash's exuberant mistress, Juliana Popjoy.

Without patronage it would have been difficult for Wood to break into the local circle. Fortunately for him, his work in London had brought him to the notice of James Brydges, Duke of Chandos. Chandos was looking for someone to help him with a scheme inspired by his visit to Bath in 1726. Finding that the lodgings he had taken near the Cross Bath left much to be desired, he foresaw that when Bath became fashionable, as he was sure it would, then anyone able to provide good, clean accommodation would be able to turn a tidy profit. Already extremely rich, he saw the chance to add to his wealth. The collaborator he finally chose, after rejecting more established architects, was John Wood.

It proved to be an uneasy partnership. Wood had his head full of grand ideas on architecture, which at this stage were not matched by his skill in building. The Duke, on the other hand, simply wanted fashionable, modern lodgings built as economically as possible.

The area to be developed was around St John's Hospital, the city's oldest charity. It was founded in the twelfth century for the care of the elderly and infirm poor people of Bath. It is unclear whether this originally included visitors to the city, but if it did this aspect of care had declined. By the sixteenth century the charity was concentrating on local needs. It was conveniently close to the Cross Bath, where aching limbs could be eased with a soak in the mineral waters. The hospital buildings, with other properties belonging to the charity, stood around a courtyard where, some ten years earlier, Killigrew had built a new chapel for the inhabitants. John Wood was disparaging about Killigrew, although the chapel has stood the test of time. Simply having another architect's work on 'his' site was enough to make Wood angry. Worse, Chandos had earlier called in the Bristol architect John Strahan to make surveys, the results of which Wood was compelled to use. The whole thing, grumbled Wood, was planned by someone else, who 'through

RIGHT The courtyard of St John's Hospital. The arches were possibly from the old building and reused by Wood in his remodelling. The first floor window to the right of the drainpipe was once a doorway, accessed by an external staircase.

BELOW The chapel at St John's is dedicated to St Michael, recalling the lost chapel of St Michael Within. St Michael is portrayed here in this nineteenth-century window in the chapel.

carelessness or incapacity took such a false survey of the land there is scarce a right angle in the whole building'. Wood was hardly in a position to accuse another of incapacity. Not only were there frequent complaints about the workmanship, but a further complication arose which was to cause endless trouble. The Duke decided to have water closets installed in his lodgings. These had not long been invented and Wood proved hopeless at fitting them. There were constant objections to the smell, which arose because Wood simply connected the down pipes straight into the town sewer. Both partners must have become disenchanted with the enterprise. Today, the courtyard is still rather muddled, although it has a quiet charm. All of the properties are now part of the hospital, although only a small part of it, standing behind a colonnade, was the hospital in Wood's day. Then there were only twelve inhabitants. Today the charity's stated aim is to provide accommodation for about a hundred residents 'who are poor persons of not less than fifty-five years old, who are inhabitants or ratepayers of the City of Bath'.

Wood must have been impatient to finish work at St John's. He already had more ambitious schemes in mind: he had been buying up the leases on farmland immediately north-west of the old city and here he planned to show off the latest architectural ideas by building formal arrangements of houses instead of simply constructing new streets or inserting new houses into old streets. The favoured shape in the early part of the eighteenth century was the square, inspired, perhaps, by Italian piazzas or palace courtyards. Wood himself, in his *Description of Bath*, describes the intention behind the building of his first great work, Queen

ABOVE Looking westwards across the gardens in Queen Square. In Wood's design, the obelisk stood in a pool of water, surrounded by formal gardens. On the west side were three Palladian villas (actually eight houses) and in the left corner the chapel of St Mary closed the vista.

OPPOSITE, TOP The grotesque carving on one of the door-cases commissioned by Earl Tylney. Compare that with

OPPOSITE, BOTTOM a Palladian grotesque on 41 Gay Street, one of the houses over which Wood had complete control.

Square, named as a tribute to Queen Caroline, the wife of George II.

His plan was for the north side of his square to have 'the elegance and grandeur of the body of a stately palace'. The other three sides were to be built in a plainer but still strictly Palladian style, to resemble the office wings of the palace. Wood, ever the architectural perfectionist, broke with the usual system of inviting local builders to take up leases to build individual houses within the overall scheme, only the exterior being in accordance with the architect's plan. Instead he placed a single mason, Samuel Eames, in charge of all the stonework, to ensure regularity. This meant, however, that instead of relying on builders to finance their own efforts, Wood had to find people prepared to take up leases for the scheme at an early stage to provide financial backing. Some of Wood's lessees proved to be strong-minded people with views of their own on architecture, and this was to cause him unforeseen difficulties. In future developments he and his son reverted to the old system, though they usually employed someone they could trust to build the first house.

As so often with Wood, his original plans did not quite come to fruition. The palace façade on the north side was built, as a grand front to a group of seven lodging houses. The south side also followed the original plan. Elsewhere details slipped from Wood's grasp. The site was to have been levelled, but, as he explains himself in the *Description of Bath*, this would have cost £4000, which he could not afford. Nor could he spare the time to try to get further investors, because, as we shall see, other squares by other architects

were already in the planning stage. He also rather coyly explains that he found himself 'under a necessity of dispensing with an uniform building for the west side of the square'. What he does not tell us is that this was not his own choice but was forced on him by two of his investors, Sir John Buckworth and Mr Greville. It was to please them that he designed what looked like three great Palladian villas. This disguised the fact that there were actually three houses in each of the end villas and two in the middle villa, which was set back from the others and had a garden at the front. The two middle houses were occupied by Buckworth and Greville. We can only imagine what this arrangement looked like from pictures of the day, for in 1830, when Palladian architecture was considered totally outdated, it was torn down, and a Greek Revival building by the Bath architect John Pinch the Younger was inserted between the other two. Although it is a fine building, it sits unhappily between its Palladian neighbours.

Nevertheless, the breaking of the western side into three houses was in some ways more successful than what happened on the east side, which was the weakest architectural composition of the four. This was due to Wood's failure, enforced by lack of money, to level the ground: the five individual houses simply step their way up the hill. One of the backers for the east side was Richard Child, Earl Tylney, who insisted on having baroque grotesques carved on the door-cases of his houses. John Wood must have hated this crude ornamentation, and the classically inspired satyr's head a few doors away at 41 Gay

Street, a house under Wood's control, may have been intended as a reproach. Today the east side serves as an object lesson in the importance of proportion in Palladian architecture. In Georgian buildings a house, its windows and the individual panes were all in related proportions, but during the nineteenth century the windows were often lengthened and the glazing bars removed. In recent years two of the houses on the east side have had their windows restored, but subsequently English Heritage – who have planning jurisdiction over these listed buildings – decided that such alterations are part of the continuing history of a house and they refuse to allow more restoration. A third house, sitting between the other two, therefore retains the Victorian fenestration. Not only do the windows look narrower than the ones on each side – which they are not – but the whole house looks narrower, although it is exactly the same width as its neighbours.

The demolition of Wood's chapel in the south-west corner and the replacement of the formal gardens have been a severe loss to Queen Square. The chapel, built in 1732 for the residents of the square, was the first of Bath's proprietary chapels. These were churches built as a commercial venture, with shareholders looking to make a profit. The ever-practical Georgians were not above using religion to their financial advantage. Wood's church is often compared with St Paul's, Covent Garden, designed in 1631 by Inigo Jones, but, like the villas on the west side of the square and the palace on the north side, it was closer in style to some buildings designed by Palladio himself. It survived until 1875, when the Midland Railway wanted to create better access for their new station at Green Park. The only exit from the south-west corner of the square was a narrow footway, so the chapel came down, together with other buildings in the street. One, which had been a large inn called the Elephant and Castle, was almost certainly another John Wood building. Not for the first or last time, some of Bath's fine buildings were sacrificed to the demands of traffic. Only the name of the street, Chapel Row, reminds us of what once stood here.

The Victorians were also responsible for the destruction of the formal gardens in the centre of the square. While the tree-planted green which replaced them is pleasant enough, it has none of their dramatic effect. Wood carefully planned the gardens to enhance the square. The gardens were surrounded by a stone balustrade with entrances in each side, rather than the present encircling railings with just one way in. Within the walls were flower borders, and four formal

ABOVE Two details from buildings in Queen Square.

TOP One of the second-floor windows. Light was sacrificed to Palladian principles.

BOTTOM Some of the rusticated stonework, with a keystone above a window.

LEFT The palace front of the north side of Queen Square, described in the latest Pevsner guide as 'one of the grandest Palladian compositions in England designed before 1730'.

LEFT, TOP Queen Square in the springtime: a view of the late-Georgian addition on the west side; and, through pink blossom, the canopy added to John Wood's own house on the south side when it became the Francis Hotel in the second half of the nineteenth century.

LEFT, BOTTOM Another view of the south side of the square. Jane Austen stayed with her brother Edward in the end house in 1799.

RIGHT On the west side of the square, John Pinch the Younger's Greek Revival building of 1830 and John Wood's Palladian villa of a century earlier sit uneasily together, although they are both fine architectural designs.

ABOVE As the leaves fall, Wood's magnificent palace front becomes visible across the square. This palace was, however, built simply as a façade for lodging-houses.

areas planted with flowering shrubs and separated by espaliers of elms and limes. The paths were turfed, and the central obelisk was surrounded by a pond. This obelisk, erected at the behest of Richard Nash to commemorate the visit of Frederick, Prince of Wales in 1738, does remain. It was originally 70 feet (21 metres) high and went to a needle point. After it was damaged in a storm in 1815 the top was chamfered into the more normal shape for obelisks. Nash pestered the poet Alexander Pope to provide a suitably grand inscription. This simple task seemed to give the literary lion writer's block and all he finally came up with was:

IN MEMORY
OF HONOURS CONFERR'D
AND IN GRATITUDE
FOR BENEFITS BESTOW'D
IN THIS CITY
BY HIS ROYAL HIGHNESS FREDERICK
PRINCE OF WALES
AND HIS
ROYAL CONSORT
IN THE YEAR MDCCXXXVIII
THIS OBELISK IS ERECTED
BY RICHARD NASH ESQ

Which is succinct and accurate, if pedestrian.

When they were first built, the houses in Queen Square were regarded as the best lodgings in Bath. Many had a communal parlour on the ground floor, with rooms let out by the floor. This is one of the reasons why the buildings have divided so readily into flats. The Reverend John Penrose, visiting in 1766, noted that the houses all had tablets over the door, advertising rooms to let. At that time Dr William Oliver, inventor of the Bath Oliver biscuit, owned no less than three houses in the square. These were the three in the northernmost villa on the west side, one of which he used as his town house. Oliver was another of the many entrepreneurs who made their fortune from the tourism boom in eighteenth-century Bath. His various enterprises as consulting physician, spa-owner, biscuit-maker and lodging-house keeper had made him very wealthy.

By the early nineteenth century Bath was becoming decidedly *passé* as far as the fashionable set were concerned, and houses built in 1730 were considered totally outdated. In her novel *Persuasion*, written in 1815–16, Jane Austen has her characters decry Queen Square for that reason. However, the Austen family had actually liked the square; Jane, with her mother and her brother Edward, stayed in No. 13 in 1799. In 1801, when looking for a permanent home in the city, Jane remarked that 'My mother hankers after the Square dreadfully.' Today she might be less enthusiastic, for Wood's palace

courtyard has become a traffic island. The peace and quiet of
this contrived stage set, intended to turn tourists into courtiers
and lodgings into mansions, has been lost. Perhaps one day
there will be a Corporation courageous enough to return the
square to pedestrians and restore the formal gardens.

South of Queen Square are two attempts by John
Strahan at a similar formal design, Beaufort and Kingsmead
Squares. Both were built as Wood was finishing Queen
Square, and he was scornful of them both, describing their
architecture as piratical. He poked fun at Strahan's inability
to control his builders in Kingsmead Square, which resulted
in a medley of styles, sizes and shapes. This, even now, can
be seen to have been an accurate criticism, but it was rather
unfair of Wood to describe Beaufort Square as having
nothing more than a sort of regularity to commend it.
Strahan's houses, though less grand than Wood's, are
attractive. Originally the square had no buildings on the
south side, so there was a view over Kingsmead to the hills
beyond, but in 1805 Bath's Theatre Royal moved from its
home in the south-east of the city to fill the gap. Its
magnificent façade facing the square, designed by the
London architect George Dance, was originally the main
entrance. After a disastrous fire at the theatre in 1862, the
main entrance was moved to the other side of the theatre, so
this delightful frontage is now rather forgotten.

South of Kingsmead Square, Strahan built Avon Street,
leading down to the river over fields known as the Ambury.
By 1736 there were twenty-five rather grand houses in the
street but the problem of flooding was already becoming
apparent. Extra houses began to be squeezed in. The far end
of the street, near the quays, was not even residential, but
just a collection of stables and warehouses. Over the years
the properties became more and more run down, with
poverty-stricken lodgers in every room of every house that
was not a brothel or a pub.

The poor of Avon Street were very poor indeed. The
euphemism 'the nymphs of Avon Street' hid a miserable
existence. There is evidence that many of these girls were
servants who had been seduced by a son of the household.
Apprentices to milliners and dressmakers also seem to have
been regarded as fair game. The story of Frances Dayer,
recorded in the Coroner's reports, will stand for many.
Evidently a troubled girl, she was thrown out of the family
home. Soon she could be found soliciting men in pubs
before taking them back to a room in Avon Street. One
evening, depressed and drunk, she threw herself in the river.
She was eighteen years old.

Most of this street, whose development started amid
such high hopes but which harboured so much misery, was
pulled down in the 1960s. Today, visitors disgorge from

LEFT In the sumptuous interior refurbishment of the Theatre Royal in 1982, under the direction of Carl Toms, the ceiling of the main auditorium was repainted as it was in 1862. It is lit by this magnificent chandelier.

BELOW, TOP The Italianate Victorian porch, now the main entrance to the theatre. Behind it can be seen Beau Nash's house, where he lived between 1720 and 1735.

BELOW, BOTTOM George III's coat of arms above the Beaufort Square façade. It was he who granted the patent to the Bath Theatre to use the title 'Royal'.

BELOW, RIGHT Here once stood the Theatre Tavern. It was replaced by this building, the church hall of the evangelical church of St Paul. This in its turn became a cinema. At left is the entrance to the Ustinov Theatre, a small modern auditorium, part of the Theatre Royal complex.

OPPOSITE, TOP The Good Samaritan carved in the tympanum of the pediment of the Victorian extension to the Royal National Hospital for Rheumatic Diseases (the Royal Mineral Water Hospital) indicates its charitable origins.

OPPOSITE, BOTTOM The parable was to have been included in the pediment of the John Wood building begun in 1738, but financial restrictions meant it was omitted. The royal coat of arms was added in the late nineteenth century.

coaches where Frances and her friends plied a miserable trade and pigs rooted around in the back gardens.

While others were imitating Wood, he was pursuing new plans. One enterprise was the building of a hospital for the care of 'poor lepers, cripples and other indigent persons resorting to Bath for cure'. In 1723 a subscription had been successful in raising money for such a hospital and Wood was commissioned to produce designs. Difficulty in finding a site delayed the scheme for many years, but when public playhouses were suppressed by law in 1737 the supporters of the hospital were able to acquire the Bath playhouse, on Upper Borough Walls, and building began on that site in 1738. Wood made the hospital a free gift of his plans and his direction of the work, while Ralph Allen supplied at no charge all the stone required for the building. The General Hospital, as it was first called, had the support of most of Bath's leading citizens. Nash, for instance, was an enthusiastic fund-raiser. Nearly a fifth of the funds available in 1742, when the hospital took its first patients, were produced by his efforts. Dr Oliver gave his services free. At first the hospital was devoted to the care of those who lived outside the city of Bath; this rule was rescinded in 1835. In its early years known as the Mineral Water Hospital, then as the Royal Mineral Water Hospital, from 1935 it has been officially called the Royal National Hospital for Rheumatic Diseases. Locally,

however, it is still affectionately known as 'The Min'. It is now one of the world's leading hospitals for the treatment of arthritic and rheumatic conditions.

In 1739, the Duke of Kingston employed Wood to design new houses for his lands on the south side of Bath, which had previously been abbey property. To avoid the flood problems faced by Strahan's houses on the Ambury, Wood raised his houses up on arches above the low-lying Abbey Orchard. Wood's development, known as the Parades, faced the earliest set of Assembly Rooms and was near the Baths, Abbey and Pump Room. Hence the houses became popular lodgings. A stroll along the wide, well-paved Parades, engaging in small talk with acquaintances, slipping secret messages to lovers, and destroying reputations, became a vital part of Bath's social life, known, appropriately, as parading. Yet here too Wood was cheated of the effect he was seeking. His original designs were far more elaborate than the final result. Angrily he wrote, in the *Description of Bath*, that one of the tenants persuaded the others to accept a reduction in costs, 'to lay aside the ornaments, to alter the proportion of the walk, and to erect the terrace walk with rubble stone'. This scheme was carried through 'to the destruction of a design, which, on paper, has given pleasure to multitudes'.

It seems likely that this penny-pinching tenant was none other than Wood's patron Ralph Allen. Allen is sometimes

said to have been the model for Squire Allworthy in Henry Fielding's most famous work, *Tom Jones*. Fielding and his sister were recipients of Allen's charity as well as being friends, and his depiction of a kindly, God-fearing man is slightly rosy. Allen had those virtues, but he was also a shrewd and at times very tough operator. Always watching out for new sources of income, he had backed the opening up of the River Avon in 1727, seeing its potential for shipping local goods to a wider market. Two years earlier the young John Wood had sent Ralph Allen some ideas he had for the improvement of Bath, which had included building the river navigation. Allen, liking the plans, interested himself in the possibilities of Bath stone. The quarries had traditionally been opencast and many were at Combe Down, on the hilltop to the south of Widcombe. In 1726 Allen began purchasing land not only in Combe Down but also at Bathampton, east of the city, which would give him control of the local stone industry.

On Wood's return to his native city in 1727, the enthusiastic young architect must have been delighted to be taken up by Ralph Allen. He was immediately offered his first commission, to build an extension to Allen's house in Lilliput Alley. Although Wood mentions this in his *Description of Bath*, he does not trumpet its virtues with his usual gusto. The extension is rather baroque in style, as were many of the grand houses in the city centre: the few that now remain include Nash's house in the Sawclose, Wolfe's House in Trim Street, Rosewell House in Kingsmead Square and 14–15 Westgate Street. Wood, ever the Palladian purist, may have been rather ashamed of it. However, Allen was later to have a much more interesting commission to offer. He decided to build a house at Widcombe, south of the city. This was intended not only to provide him with a grand home suitable to his status, but also to show off the durability of Bath stone to sceptical London builders, who compared it to 'Cheshire cheese, liable to breed maggots that would soon devour it'.

Perhaps this is the moment to consider Bath stone. It was formed during the Jurassic period, around 190 million years ago. At the time when the sediments were being laid down beneath the sea, the constantly moving water was not conducive to marine life, and it is largely free of fossils, although other strata in the same quarry are often rich in them. It therefore has a very even appearance, which is said to resemble fish roe, hence the name oolite, from two Greek words meaning egg and stone. At first it seems to have a very homogeneous colour, but there are distinct variations between the different quarries. A good stonemason can identify the various stones simply by their colour and texture. Before being inserted into a building it should be 'seasoned' – left in a dry place while it dries out. With some structural

exceptions, it should lie in the building the same way it lay in the quarry. When newly quarried it is very white, which is why Jane Austen complained about the glare. Over time it mellows to the characteristic honey colour.

Not all the stone that can be seen around Bath is Bath stone. The rougher material which is often used for the backs of buildings and for garden walls is from the same quarries, but it is not Bath stone. Although inferior in appearance, it is actually a tougher material than oolite. Another stone that is often seen locally is lias. This white or grey stone is found in early buildings. An old house in the Sawclose which dates from 1625 is constructed of it, though with Bath stone quoins.

Bath stone has been cut from the ground from Roman times onwards. Some blocks were recycled. There may well be stones in Georgian buildings in Bath that were first quarried by the Romans, rescued by the Saxons, and then cut and used over and over again as the town altered. Originally the quarrying was open-cast, but as time wore on it literally went underground. Today these vast caverns have been christened 'stone mines', a term heartily despised by quarrymen. The fact that they lie beneath the village of Combe Down has led to years of anxiety for homeowners while people argue over what to do about them. Here and there some houses have shown signs of subsidence.

However, these are always modern houses. The old masons who made their homes there from Ralph Allen's day onwards knew where the caverns were and they did not build over them. There is now a scheme to stabilize them and at the same time to preserve some of the history. A visit to the caverns is a strange and moving experience. However, no one should try to enter without the presence of a guide and the permission of the landowner.

Anyone wishing to explore the remains of open-cast quarrying should follow the National Trust's Skyline Walk, in the area known as Bathampton Rocks. There are traces of the tramway which took the stone from these quarries to the Kennet and Avon Canal down in the valley below. A geological trail can be followed at Monkton Farleigh, in the Brown's Folly nature reserve. Slightly further afield, at Box, there are footpaths which lead through the quarries near Hazelbury. But the best way to see Bath stone is simply to walk through the city.

Back in the early eighteenth century, however, even Ralph Allen could not know how fashionable the stone would become. He began acquiring property in Widcombe from 1728 onwards. At that time the old village, clustered around the parish church, was a semi-rural suburb where wealthy citizens had little villas. The only substantial house before Ralph Allen moved there was Widcombe Manor, a

BATH STONE

LEFT This detail of a scroll carved in Bath stone shows the tiny, nearly spherical particles called ooids, derived from the Greek word for egg because they resemble fish eggs. Thus Bath stone is known as oolite.

RIGHT, CLOCKWISE FROM TOP LEFT This carved plaque shows the evenness of top-quality Bath stone. Ooolite is a 'freestone' – it can be carved in any direction, as this tight scrollwork demonstrates. The colour can vary from a deep honey colour to pale cream.

ABOVE, LEFT The south front of Widcombe Manor.

ABOVE, RIGHT Widcombe Manor seen from the west, with the parish church beside it. This rural scene is only a mile from the city centre.

OPPOSITE The tower of Widcombe parish church, dedicated to St Thomas à Becket, provides a backdrop for a fifteenth-century Italian fountain, installed some time in the mid-twentieth century. This exotic import, with its gambolling baby satyrs, sits very happily in the courtyard of an English country manor house.

Jacobean house which received a Georgian makeover about 1730. The neighbouring village of Lyncombe was, according to John Wood, then in decline, its old houses standing empty and deserted. However, cold-water springs were discovered there in 1737, and by 1742 these had been developed, along with a lodging house, gardens and pump room. Known as Lyncombe Spa, it became a popular rural retreat for visitors weary of the hustle and bustle of Bath. There was also another village, named Holloway, squeezed between the River Avon to the north and Beechen Cliff to the south.

Ralph Allen's arrival was to bring a profound change to the quiet valleys of Widcombe and Lyncombe. Allen's investment in the stone quarries of Combe Down (then known simply as Combe) led to a revolution in quarrying and building practices in the city. Hitherto, masons had been employed, lucratively, on piecework. As the blocks were cut from the quarry, they were worked by the highly skilled free masons. (These craftsmen should not be confused with the secret society of the Freemasons, although the latter organization was born out of the medieval guild of the free masons.) When the work was finished, the blocks were sent on, by cart, to the rough masons, who incorporated them into the buildings for which they were intended. This meant that finely carved ornaments and sharply cut blocks were often damaged before they reached the building.

Allen was not prepared to tolerate this inefficient and restrictive practice. Again we see the other side of his character, that of the tough, uncompromising businessman. By 1740, with Wood's co-operation, he had broken the independence of the stonemasons, bringing the cost of stone and labour tumbling. Allen insisted that his masons should be regular employees. When the local masons objected and refused to work for him, Wood imported blackleg labour from Yorkshire. In return for the commitment to regular employment, however, Allen provided tied cottages near the quarries and at the wharf. Designed by Wood and built by Allen's Clerk of Works, Richard Jones, they were of such high quality that they are still desirable homes today. At Combe Down the foreman's house even had a chapel for the spiritual welfare of the workers. Furthermore, although he cut the hourly rate of pay, Allen ensured a constant supply of work, so that the men found they were better off than before.

Allen also revolutionized transportation. From 1731 stone cut from the quarry was taken directly to the riverbank by a tramway, designed, at Allen's instigation, by the Bristol engineer John Padmore and based on those in coalmines in northern England. Each truck carried several blocks of stone, and was controlled by a brakeman as it descended by gravity. Given the length and steepness of the hill it was

LEFT AND ABOVE In his palace of Prior Park, Ralph Allen could see the city laid out before him. The east wing was by Allen's Clerk of Works, Richard Jones.

probably quite an exciting ride. The empty trucks were towed back up by horses. At the wharf, Padmore also built a crane for transferring large blocks of stone to barges for shipping to other parts of the country via the newly navigable river. Meanwhile, the stone for Bath was worked in purpose-built sheds, protecting both men and stone from the weather. The tramway was dismantled in 1764, after Ralph Allen's death, but the crane remained in service. Both were a great source of wonder and admiration to visitors.

It was on ground alongside the tramway, at the head of the valley, that Ralph Allen decided to build his great mansion. Once again, John Wood found himself in the employ of a wealthy patron who was not prepared to invest that wealth to fulfil his architect's dreams. Moreover, Allen had men working for him, notably Richard Jones, who were quite capable of taking over from Wood if things went wrong. And, inevitably, they did. At first it seemed that Wood and Allen were in agreement that the house would be a celebration of local stone. The floors as well as the walls were to be constructed of Bath stone. Instead of plasterwork decorations, there would be stone. Wood had even designed an entrance where visitors would be able to admire carved ornaments. It sounds rather like a statuary showroom. But as quickly as Wood proposed plans, Allen changed them. It seems he soon decided that comfort and

economy were to be preferred to lavish display. Wood's *Description of Bath* gives us an idea of how it should have looked, but, as Wood remarks, the stone ornaments in the parlour and dining room were cut off, and the walls were wood-lined. Only the chapel, in the east wing of the house, gives us some idea of Wood's brilliance.

One cannot help but sympathize with Allen as he looked at his chilly palace. Externally it was (and is) as magnificent as he could have wished. It can be seen from the city centre, and visitors and citizens alike must have felt that there indeed lived a prince among men. Unfortunately, despite the best efforts of Richard Jones and Ralph Allen, the main block, while grand on the outside, was dark and cramped within. Pierce Egan, writing in 1819, described it as 'the comfortless palace of Prior Park'.

However lacking in comfort Prior Park may have been, Allen and his wife took possession in 1741 and were able to attract to their new home a coterie of interesting friends, among them Alexander Pope. Although the poet was later to bite the kindly hand that not only fed him but also provided the roof over his head during his visits to Bath, he did help Allen to design the gardens. Among Pope's friends were the owners of the three great landscape gardens of the day, Stowe, Rousham and Cirencester. The gardens at Prior Park include elements of them all: a grotto, temples, false canals and, most famously, the Palladian Bridge. This was based on the one at Stowe, which in its turn was a copy of that at Wilton. Allen even erected, on a neighbouring hillside, a sham castle, designed for him by Sanderson Miller. Unlike the ones at Stowe or Cirencester, it had no cottages behind it – it is simply a wall. Even odder, it cannot be seen from Prior Park. It was built as an eye-catcher to delight and amuse the visitors to the city, a function it still performs today. After years of neglect, the grounds of Prior Park are now in the hands of the National Trust, who are restoring them to some semblance of their former glory.

Ralph Allen's tramway was only the first of many forms of transport that brought upheaval to Widcombe. In October 1794 work began on a canal to link London and Bristol. It was to take in the existing Kennet Navigation from Reading to Newbury and the Avon Navigation from Bath to Bristol. In 1795 the shareholders of the Avon Navigation

Company seemed about to refuse to collaborate with this scheme, so the Kennet and Avon Canal Company decided to continue the canal through to Bristol. Surveys were taken. In the meantime, however, the Canal Company quietly acquired shares in the Avon Navigation and by 1796 they had control. The Bristol canal scheme was dropped and a flight of locks was built to bring the canal down to the river at Widcombe.

From 1810, when the Kennet and Avon Canal was completed, there was constant traffic of narrowboats with their thirsty crews through Widcombe. They were not the only travellers passing through this once quiet village. Carts and mule trains, heading for the quays or bringing merchandise to the flourishing city, came down the steep hill, following old pack routes, or along the Lower Bristol Road. The drovers, carriers and footsore pedestrians, like the boatmen, were ready for refreshment. Naturally there were plenty of inns and alehouses to cater for them.

RIGHT Pitt the Elder, one of Allen's guests at Prior Park, suggested that he should build a sham castle – in reality just a wall; it was also Pitt who put Allen in touch with Sanderson Miller, who designed the castle.

OPPOSITE The grounds of Crowe Hall were designed for the Tugwell family in 1874 by William Carmichael, Head Gardener at Sandringham. They give a fine view of Prior Park. The house, first built in the eighteenth century, has since been reconstructed several times.

LEFT AND RIGHT The flight of
steps in front of the great portico
of Prior Park was an inspired
nineteenth-century addition.

By 1800, the population of Lyncombe and Widcombe stood at three thousand. Thirty years later the figure had trebled. Included in the 1830 count were close to six hundred weavers. The village was now an important wool town. It was also, in parts, something of a thieves' kitchen, for the parish had no police force.

Cheap housing had sprung up on the low-lying area known as Dolemeads, an area which acquired the nickname of Mud Island, on account of its propensity to flood. One harrowing description, written during the floods of 1841, describes the state of the houses: 'The inhabitants were seen occupying them, wet as they were, without a spark of fire and exposed to the cold wind, making its way through the broken windows, from which the rags which stopped them up had been washed by the flood.' Finally, in the early 1900s, an estate of model houses was erected, which kept the community together while improving their conditions beyond measure. These homes have survived to the present day, although it was the 1970s before the threat of catastrophic flooding was lifted.

Another transport-led change came to Widcombe in 1840, when Brunel brought the Great Western Railway to Bath. Avoiding the great Georgian architectural gems, the railway carved its way through the southern suburbs. One of Brunel's ideas was to put the whole of Claverton Street in a

tunnel. Not surprisingly, this met with a certain amount of disfavour. Yet even the final solution was hardly an enhancement to Widcombe. Bath itself gained a Jacobean station with a Tudor-style viaduct, both constructed in best Bath stone. However, the back of the station was much plainer, and the south side of the viaduct was built of poor-quality stone and brick. This was considered good enough for working-class Widcombe.

Road transport has wreaked havoc here too. Houses were pulled down for road widening as early as 1825, with another scheme in 1852. But it was in the 1960s that Rossiter Road, much reviled by present inhabitants, was built along the south side of the river, destroying buildings including Thomas Greenway's Cold Bath and some pleasant Georgian artisan housing.

Further development on the south side of Bath was slow and patchy. Apart from the lower slopes of Holloway, where houses of all types, from mansions to hovels, clung to the hillside, the fields beyond Widcombe remained largely rural until the late nineteenth century. Halfway up Holloway was (and still is) the little chapel of St Mary Magdalen. There too are the remnants of the medieval Leper Hospital, rebuilt in 1761 when it was the Home for Imbecile Children. Just below it is an attractive Georgian house which today is a guest house, but most of the buildings were torn down in

LEFT The view northwards from Beechen Cliff.

the 1960s to be replaced by the comfortable but utilitarian Calton Buildings. At the top of Holloway was a large inn called the Bear, which stood on Bear Flat (both so called after the local word for barley, rather than the animal). It was owned by Ralph Allen and provided the first stop for thirsty travellers *en route* for Wells, Exeter or Falmouth. It seems probable that stagecoach passengers walked up Holloway, as this was standard practice on the steepest hills, to spare the horses.

In the late Georgian period a few speculative builders erected terraces such as Devonshire Buildings and Bloomfield Place above Bear Flat but the area remained unspoilt farmland for many years, with just the annual horse fair to enliven proceedings. It did this so effectively that in 1836 the Corporation set up a committee to control or stop it, as it was inconvenient and encouraged immorality. This objective was evidently achieved, for by 1840 the local newspaper reported that it was so poorly supported it was 'only a shade above being no fair at all'.

Beechen Cliff, high above the river, has been a fashionable tourist spot since the eighteenth century. In Jane Austen's day it was somewhere to come and admire the view – as well as a popular place to burn effigies of hated public figures. The Victorians and Edwardians felt no visit to Bath was complete without a trip to this viewpoint. Early postcards show an apparently limitless number of panoramic views from Beechen Cliff. The late Victorians decided it was a salubrious spot for homes, and a family of Methodist builders developed an estate of terraced houses, the streets being named after poets such as Shakespeare, Longfellow and (somewhat surprisingly) Byron. Today the area is known as Poets' Corner.

And so the southern fringes of Bath became filled with housing. Farms, fields, brickworks and nurseries have, over the last hundred years, quietly disappeared under a creeping tide of homes of all types. Here and there traces remain. Alleyways, known locally as drungways, run behind and between gardens: they are the remnants of old pack routes and field footpaths. Old cottages are revamped, and here and there what were once farm buildings now serve as garages. But if modern Bath has moved southward, the Georgian builders looked north and began to scale the slopes of Lansdown and Camden.

A TEMPLE TO ANTIQUITY

THE KING'S CIRCUS & JOHN WOOD'S PLANS FOR BATH

A TEMPLE TO ANTIQUITY

THE KING'S CIRCUS & JOHN WOOD'S PLANS FOR BATH

As Bath's popularity continued to grow, more and more entrepreneurs of all kinds began to interest themselves in the city. Landowners rubbed their hands at the thought that former pastureland might yield a new crop – ground rent. Speculative builders, sometimes dubiously financed, queued to erect the developments being proposed by architects both professional and amateur. They, in their turn, saw a chance to try out their latest designs, bending and stretching the rules laid down by Palladio. It is ironic that while the modern city has strict planning regulations to protect the old, the old itself was a series of unconnected developments governed only by the rules of taste.

Only one man harboured a vision for the entire city. That man was John Wood. He was a dreamer, a visionary, if an irascible one. His head was full of Celtic myths, classical learning and biblical tales, which he succeeded in combining to prove that Bath was Trinovantum – the new Troy. He believed firmly that those Trojans who had escaped the sack of their city had settled in the green and pleasant valley that was his home. In his attempt to show that Bath was founded long before the Romans came, he referred to the building of Solomon's temple, the prophet David and the story of Romulus and Remus. He was fascinated by stone circles such as Stonehenge, his interest partly inspired by his hero, Inigo Jones, who had published, by Royal Command, a study of

Stonehenge, which he had decided was the remains of a Roman temple of the Tuscan order. Wood's curiosity was much aroused by the ring at Stanton Drew, south of Bristol. He was convinced that the 'Drew' was a Druid temple, perhaps even a university, where students were instructed in the Liberal Sciences. But he was even more intrigued by the Roman remains constantly being uncovered as new building developments spread through and beyond the old city and the busy spades of the workmen turned over long-unbroken ground.

All these ideas eventually came together in his head in a startling concept for the city. If ancient Bath – Akemancester – had been the new Troy, then he, John Wood, would create a new Rome in its place. 'I proposed,' he wrote, ' to take an exact plan of the city and after laying out the whole in a regular manner, every person that should take a new lease of any of the Chamber [i.e. the Coporation's] lands and tenements was to covenant to build nothing but what should be conformable to it.'

In the 1743 edition of his *Essay towards a Description of Bath* he proposed a huge forum on the riverside area known as the Ham, the flood plain on the south-east side of the city, between the city wall and the river. He was adamant that the Roman forum, where the people would have celebrated their feasts and festivals and carried on their commerce, had been

ABOVE The Circus from the air. The Assembly Rooms can be seen to the right.

on this site. His forum would be even grander. He planned to tame the River Avon and open it out into an 'Octangular Bason'. This would act as the haven, or harbour, for boats bringing goods to Bath by water. There were to be colonnaded piazzas on each bank with bridges spanning the river. It was to have 'an air of magnificence, equal to anything of its kind'. This was only the beginning. He also proposed to build an Imperial Gymnasium, combining leisure facilities with new hot baths for invalids. The modern spa complex is finally fulfilling that aim, a stone's throw from Wood's original site. Alas, Bath has had to wait 260 years for his dream to come true, for his plans soon came to grief.

First to go was the Royal Forum. Even before the first edition of the *Description of Bath* was published he knew he was running into trouble. In an effort to persuade people to go along with his plans for the city, he pointed out that he was laying aside his cherished plans for Queen Square as a sacrifice to the greater good of co-ordinated planning. Although this won over some councillors, others, he wrote angrily, 'thought proper to treat my schemes as chimerical'. He resolved to pursue plans for developments of his own in fields on the north-west of the city and on the Abbey Orchard, which lay just north of the Ham, although at that stage he had not abandoned the Royal Forum. However, by the next edition of the *Description* in 1749 the Royal Forum

plans had been dropped. The site is still largely under-developed. In the place of Wood's piazzas there is only a rather unsightly car park.

Wood made various attempts to build his Imperial Gymnasium. Undaunted by the failure of his first tentative plans, he incorporated the idea of a circular building in his first designs for the General Hospital. This was to be a structure 70 feet (21 metres) in diameter. Lukewarm water would be pumped from the King's Bath for treatments. When Wood published a plan of the city in 1736, possibly in celebration of his achievements so far, he was so certain the plans were settled that he indicated the new circular General Hospital on its proposed site just south of the city wall. He should have waited. The landowner (and co-developer) took fright at the cost, and a corrupt trustee of the hospital bought the land to block the scheme. Wood did not give up. Even if the gymnasium itself eluded his grasp, he was still determined to achieve a great circular building. When he heard that the Corporation was to erect a new building for King Edward's School, he smartly put forward his latest designs. Inevitably, they included a circular court 'forty two feet in diameter, with an arcade twelve feet broad'. He did not get the job. Still he persevered. At last, in February 1754, the foundation stone of the King's Circus was laid. The realization of his dream was within his grasp.

ABOVE More views of the Circus showing LEFT the full effect of the columns and RIGHT the frieze of garlands and masks between the Corinthian columns.

PAGES 96–97 Details from the carvings of the Doric frieze. Note in particular the hand holding an oak tree, a reference to the Druids used by John Wood as a pun on his own name, and the metope of the four winds – an important picture from Withers's book *Emblems*.

Why was John Wood so desperate to erect this circular building? The Roman Colosseum was probably the initial inspiration, but gradually more complicated ideas hinging on his mystical beliefs became involved. If we look at the Circus today, using the clues that he gave us, we can understand his thinking. First, it contains references to Stonehenge. Not only is it a stone circle, but it has a diameter of what Wood called 60 cubits, that is 316 feet or 97 metres. He contrived, by massaging the figures, to find the same measurement at Stonehenge and at Stanton Drew. This measurement introduces the next clue: Solomon's temple.

Almost certainly John Wood was a Freemason, a member of the secret society formed in London in 1717. The movement spread throughout Europe and across the Atlantic to America. George Washington was one prominent Mason. Mozart was another: his opera *The Magic Flute* gives an insight into their declared aims and their ritual. Wood's membership in a Bath lodge has never been established, and it is possible that he retained allegiance to a London lodge. Certainly he was an antiquarian, and in the eighteenth century Masonic lodges and antiquarian societies were closely linked. Both had beliefs which harked back to a golden age of architecture and mathematics. Much of this centred on the building of Solomon's temple. Its height and breadth were both supposed to be the magic 60 cubits.

Within the circle of the Circus is a triangle, marked by the three entrances; draw lines between them and there it is – another Masonic symbol, the triangle in the circle, or the Trinity in Eternity.

Another striking feature of the Circus is Wood's use of the three classic orders of architecture: Doric, Ionic and Corinthian. At ground floor level is a circle of columns in the plain, strong style which some modern purists insist is not Doric but Tuscan, but which to Wood was certainly Doric. At the second level are Ionic columns, slim and graceful with scroll volutes at the top. Above these are columns in the more elaborate Corinthian style, topped with acanthus leaves. Crowning the whole edifice is a ring of acorns. Here John Wood has returned to the Druids, whose symbol of power was the oak tree, and to the story about Bladud, Bath's legendary founder, in whom Wood believed implicitly.

It is easy to get carried away by all this iconography. At times Wood almost seems to be teasing us. Above the Doric columns is a frieze with over five hundred carvings or metopes. For years the meaning of these metopes puzzled architects and historians. Some are clear references to early occupants or landlords of the houses. Others are Masonic symbols such as dividers and beehives. But what of the crocodile, the four winds or the heliotrope? These were finally traced to an illustrated children's book of the

LEFT AND BELOW The Circus comes as a complete surprise to anyone climbing up the steep slope of Gay Street. At the top, its ornamented interior bursts upon the eye, even through the plane trees.

RIGHT A detail of the frieze above the second-floor windows of the Circus.

seventeenth century. Yet no one has satisfactorily explained why Wood wanted them on the Circus. It is perhaps significant that the image of the four winds is included in the book as part of a game of chance which could be played using the pictures. Is this what it is all about? Is Wood merely playing a game? Some writers, seeking to extend the analogy with stone circles, have declared firmly that there are thirty houses, to match the thirty stones in the outer rings at Stonehenge and Stanton Drew. A quick count of the front doors appears to confirm this. But it is an illusion. There are thirty-three houses, and there always have been, as a glance at the original leases shows. The three extra ones have entrances in side streets. A trick? A trap? Or possibly an alteration by Wood's son, also an architect, and also, confusingly, called John. The Circus could originally have been planned with thirty houses, for the first segment to be built has only ten. Shortly after work began a national recession triggered by the Seven Years' War put the project on hold for nearly ten years, until the mid-1760s. One of the two later segments is made up of twelve houses, the other of eleven.

This may have been an economy measure, for John Wood the Younger was a far more practical, down-to-earth man than his father. And it was he, not John Wood the Elder, who actually built the Circus. Just three months after the foundation stone of this extraordinary building was laid,

John Wood the Elder was dead. He was forty-nine years old. He never saw his circular building, his very own temple.

Like Wood himself, the Circus was controversial. Some were enthusiastic. A guidebook of 1770 describes it as 'one of the most elegant piles of building in Europe' Others found fault. Tobias Smollett, in his novel *Humphry Clinker* (1771), has one character describe it as 'a pretty bauble, designed for show and looks like Vespasian's amphitheatre turned inside out'. It was inconvenient, the decorations were childish and misplaced, and the approach up Gay Street steep and slippery, continued Smollett's *alter ego*, Matthew Bramble. The rather fearsome Mrs Elizabeth Montagu wrote to her sister-in-law in 1779 saying that, although it appeared a good stone edifice on the outside, inside it was a nest of boxes, 'in which I should be stifled, if the masonry were not so bad as to admit winds at many places'.

Later it suffered from alterations at other hands. The little balconies were added as window guards. About 1830 its original dramatic effect was softened when the hitherto paved central area, with its circular reservoir of water, was grassed over. The reservoir was filled in and the trees were planted. The trees are London planes (*Platanus* x *hispanica*), which, with their feet in a regular supply of water, have done particularly well – to the rage of those who insist they should be cut down because you can't see the Wood for the trees.

Today the tour buses circle the King's Circus, film-makers use it as a set, and tourists struggle to find a satisfactory way to capture it in a snapshot. Despite all this, its astonishingly bold architecture still draws gasps of surprise and admiration, as it springs unexpectedly upon the eye. The odd thing about the Circus is that externally there is nothing to prepare one for the drama within. It is hidden from visitors until they actually walk in through one of the entrances. Even today, it remains a secret place, and a place of secrets.

It was John Wood the Younger who carried on his father's ambitions. As we shall see in the next chapter, he had an exciting scheme of his own, but, like his father, he ran into difficulties. His first problem was how to entice the great, the good and the fashionable into his latest buildings. They were regarded as being practically out in the country, and too far from social centres such as the Pump Room and the Assembly Rooms. While he could do nothing about bringing hot water nearer, he could build new Assembly Rooms. Even here there were problems. He needed subscribers to back the plan, and there were rivals seeking to advance their own schemes. Initially Wood chose a dramatic site, overlooking Queen Square. However, the subscribers fell out among themselves, and instead Wood built a row of houses, which he called Queen's Parade.

Eventually a garden belonging to a Mr Holdstock became available, just east of the Circus. It was far from ideal. The backs of the houses in the Circus, which overlooked it, were the usual uneven muddle, very different from the elegant frontage. The ground rose steeply to the north, and to the south other new buildings were being erected. Whether this robbed Wood of inspiration we cannot know, but the exterior is decidedly mundane – two vast stone sheds linked by a rather inadequate porch. Presumably in an attempt to give it an air of grandeur, Wood designed Alfred and Bennett Streets facing it on either side. However, they only succeed in making the site look even more cramped.

Had one of Wood's competitors won the contract for the Assembly Rooms, the result might have been something quite startling. Robert Adam, designer of great houses such as Kenwood and Osterley, submitted designs that were far more palatial – and far more expensive. Economy won the day. Seventy shares at £200 each were offered in a tontine. In its simplest form a tontine is an issue of a set number of shares, the income being allocated to the holders. As each

dies, his portion is divided among the survivors, the last survivor scooping the pool. Some schemes had refinements: certainly in the Assembly Rooms tontine the shares could be inherited. By April 1769, fifty-three of the shares had been taken up. Among the subscribers was Mr Leigh Perrot, Jane Austen's uncle, with eight shares. Another subscriber was Walter Wiltshire, a man who had made a fortune through his carrying service. He happened to be a friend of Gainsborough, who was then living in the Circus. These connections allowed Gainsborough and his friend and fellow artist Garvey to profit from the venture: Gainsborough was employed to paint and frame a portrait, and Garvey decorated the walls of the Rooms.

While externally the Rooms leave something to be desired, inside they are magnificent. In addition to the Ballroom and Tea Room there is the Octagon Room, which was originally used as a card room. However, there were so many card-players that it proved insufficient to hold them all. An extension, now the café, had to be built in 1777.

RIGHT The north side of the Assembly Rooms was designed as shops.

101

Other rooms were used as coffee and billiard rooms, and there was a ladies' withdrawing room, where a maid attended. There was accommodation for the steward and the housekeeper, with a suite of rooms for the Master of Ceremonies. There was even a cold plunge bath. Plans were mooted for an icehouse in the sedan chair court, but this seems to have come to nothing. Daytime visitors could also call into the little shops which were in an arcade on the northern side. These, regrettably, were cleared away and the arcade closed in during the 1930s, making the north side even bleaker.

The rooms, known as the New or Upper Rooms, opened on 30 September 1771. The Master of Ceremonies, Captain Wade, wanting it to be a brilliant occasion, requested those in mourning 'to appear in colour on that evening if it shall suit their convenience'. How unthinkable that request would have been a century later to the obsequy-obsessed Victorians! Soon the balls held in the Upper Rooms were part of the Bath social scene. Mr Gyde, proprietor of the Lower Rooms, clearly alarmed by the development, suggested a coalition. This proposal was rejected, but society itself dictated some sort of co-operation, so that the fashionable could attend as many events as possible. Thus public balls at the Upper Rooms were on Mondays and Thursdays, to avoid a clash with those at the Lower Rooms on Tuesdays and Fridays.

There were various teething troubles, not least with the chandeliers. The five we see today in the Ballroom are not the originals, which were made by a Mr Collett of London for the enormous sum of £400. In today's money that would be about £33,000, so we can see that, having cut back on the initial costs, no expense was now being spared. By October, however, bits began falling off them, on one occasion hitting the dancers, another time falling on Thomas Gainsborough, who was standing underneath chatting to a friend. While this sounds comical, we must remember that the branches contained lighted candles, and the ladies' hairstyles, made up as they were of lambswool, grease and other padding, were highly combustible. The Corporation called in William Parker, another London chandelier-maker, who reported back to the committee that they were 'so unsafe as to endanger the lives of the Company'. Mr Collett's servant was ordered to take them down, and Mr Collett was asked to return the money 'without putting the Committee to the disagreeable necessity of compelling you to refund it'.

Unfortunately for the committee, Mr Collett was made of sterner stuff. While Mr Parker replaced the chandeliers with the ones we see today, and supplied three more for the Tea Room at an additional cost of £330, Mr Collett ignored solicitors' letters, final warnings and appeals to his better nature. The row rumbled on for two years, until the

committee agreed that Mr Collett would make a chandelier for the Octagon for nothing, as a compromise. However not only did he use parts of the substandard chandeliers but he then had the temerity to submit a bill, pointing out that the committee had insisted on his using an exceptionally strong chain, and he had had to employ the best craftsmen to carry out the installation. The committee, exhausted by the whole affair, protested but paid up.

So let us for a moment slip back in time and imagine being bystanders at a ball at the New Assembly Rooms in the 1770s. The Ballroom is crowded, with perhaps a thousand people sitting on the benches that line the walls. Mr Parker's lustres are shimmering with the light from two hundred candles. The unfriendly night is hidden from view by blinds painted by Mr Garvey with classical figures and vases, a theme continued with statues and vases in the niches. Overseeing events is the Master of Ceremonies, Captain Wade, whose portrait by Gainsborough dominates the Octagon. The ladies who wish to dance the minuet are wearing full hoops, so that they are very wide at the hips. Each dancer has two long streamers of lace called lappets

RIGHT Detail of one of the chandeliers in the Tea Room, by William Parker of London.

hanging from her elaborate, freshly powdered hairstyle. Her partner is wearing his most elegant 'full suite of clothes or a French frock', unless he is an officer of the Army or the Navy, when he will be wearing dress uniform. These couples dance, sometimes three pairs at a time, until all those who want to show off their skills have finished. Then everyone retreats to the Tea Room, for supper.

Refreshments include savouries such as pies, tongue and anchovies, and sweetmeats such as jellies, syllabubs and madeleines. Liquid refreshment ranges from tea, coffee and lemonade to port (red and white), champagne, hock, claret, tokay, Madeira and Rhenish wine. The dancers are soon joined by the card-players, who have been playing games such as whist and piquet, with cards of the best quality. During this break the ladies wearing full hoops withdraw to remove these appendages, doubtless calling on the maid to assist. After supper come lively country dances which continue cheerfully until the magic hour of 11 p.m. Then Captain Wade commands the music to cease, the dancers reluctantly perform their final bows, and they withdraw from the Ballroom. The ladies fan themselves while their escorts try to find them sedan chairs in the mêlée outside. Slowly the revellers disperse, but not before having made arrangements for future meetings, some public, some clandestine. The steward removes the candle-ends from the lustres, the musicians put away their instruments, and silence falls. The ball is over.

It says something of the determination of eighteenth-century fashionable society to pursue entertainment that the Rooms succeeded in their early years, for visitors had to travel through not just one but several building sites to reach them. Alfred Street and Bennett Street were built in the years following the construction of the Rooms, and there was also Milsom Street to be negotiated. Now Bath's principal shopping street, it was a field, reaching down into the heart of the expanding city, until late in the eighteenth century. It was enclosed by Broad Street to the east and Queen Square to the west. Wood and his favourite builder, Samuel Eames, had built houses on the line of modern George Street as early as the 1730s. (Wood had also built a tennis court at the top of Barton Street, but this early attempt at a sports centre in Bath seems to have been a failure, for it was quickly turned into houses.) Even the construction of the Circus was well advanced by the time Charles Milsom, a wine-cooper, finally had his plans for buildings on this site approved by the Corporation. These plans included development of the

Town Acre at the top of the slope, below the site of the Upper Rooms. The land had been in the family since 1741, when Daniel Milsom, a schoolmaster, rented the ground outside the Borough Walls which then became known as Milsom's Garden. He put forward various schemes, including one for a school to be built next to a pub then called the Full Moon, but now known as Sam Weller's. His plans were blocked by the intrusion into his plot of the poorhouse for St Michael's and the Abbey. After Daniel's death in 1755, his successor, Charles, successfully renegotiated the leases and in 1761 work started. Milsom Street linked up early streets like Green Street, built on a seventeenth-century bowling green, and more recent developments like John Wood the Elder's Quiet Street, which led to Queen Square; in addition a right of way was granted through the old city wall. Unlike the Woods, the Milsoms were both councillors, and they knew how to get things past the Corporation. As well as Milsom Street the project included extensions to George Street, such as Edgar Buildings, which provides an impressive termination to the street. Prince's Buildings was added between 1764 and 1770. Most of this work had therefore been completed by the time the Assembly Rooms opened, but there must have been considerable disruption in 1780 when the old poorhouse halfway up Milsom Street was finally demolished and Somersetshire Buildings erected on the site to plans by Thomas Baldwin, the City Surveyor.

Like the rest of the street, Somersetshire Buildings was intended to be dwellings. In common with all Bath's houses at that time, they had sunken areas in front of them, guarded by railings. Businessmen, however, saw it as a good commercial site, particularly with the New Town continuing to expand to the north. They moved in, and further building work took place as house fronts were ripped out and replaced by shop windows, initially with 'flying bays' over the areas, eventually encroaching on the pavement itself. The ground floor room of the central house at Somersetshire Buildings, with its magnificent plasterwork ceiling, is now a banking hall, and has been so since the 1790s. By Jane Austen's day the street was a mixture of shops and lodgings, such as those in which she places the Tilney family in *Northanger Abbey*. The shops included milliners', print shops, confectioners', circulating libraries – all the sort of inessential but attractive shops beloved by tourists then and now.

By the early nineteenth century fashionable society, following the Prince Regent, was going to the seaside, and

the Bath described by Jane Austen was becoming quieter, staider, more respectable. As yet the signs of decline were limited. Though Jane teasingly describes one ball at the Upper Rooms as 'shockingly and inhumanly thin', she immediately qualifies this comment by adding that it would still 'have made five or six very pretty Basingstoke assemblies'. The Tea Room was still often so crowded at dances that many departed 'without partaking of that wholesome and reviving beverage'. In 1818 the Ballroom was so full that Heaviside, the Master of Ceremonies, found it almost impossible to lead off the minuet. However, there is no doubt that the city's splendours were fading. In *The Pickwick Papers* (1836–7), Charles Dickens describes a ball where 'queer old ladies and decrepid old gentlemen' intermingled with match-making mammas, flirting daughters and 'silly young men, displaying varieties of puppyism and stupidity'. In the 1840s one shopkeeper said dolefully that you could have fired a cannon up Milsom Street and not hit anyone. There were still enough people to support two concerts by Franz Liszt and his fellow musicians, one at the Theatre Royal and one at the Assembly

Rooms. At the Rooms, however, other entertainments were less up-market – General Tom Thumb and marionettes vied with more intellectual fare. Periodic redecorations of the Rooms reflected Victorian taste – dark greens, reds and ambers in 1865, replaced by pastel pinks and blues with decorative arabesques and dados in 1879. The Rooms were decorated again in 1890 when large mirrors appeared with odd circular embellishments between them. During World War I the Ballroom was used for aeroplane work, and then as the mess for the School of Aeronautics. By 1921 it had become a cinema. In 1931 the Society for the Protection of Ancient Buildings stepped in to purchase the building and by 1938 the Rooms had been restored. Four years later, on 25 April 1942, they were burnt out by incendiary bombs.

After the war arguments raged about the future of the Assembly Rooms. Should their charred remains be turned into flats, or even pulled down? Fortunately the building belonged to the National Trust and not the Corporation, and, after lengthy discussions with the War Damage Commission, work began on restoration in 1956. Today the building is one of the Georgian jewels of the city, still used for everything from concerts to weddings, with the Museum of Costume occupying the basement.

There have been other changes. The Circus is still mainly residential, although Elizabeth Montagu's nest of boxes has been further divided into flats with the odd sprinkling of dentists' surgeries. Milsom Street has undergone a controversial revamping but is still full of busy shops not unlike those Jane Austen would have known. Bath in the twenty-first century is just as ready to welcome visitors as the Bath of Beau Nash.

There are, however, quieter parts of Bath, and to discover those we must turn westwards, following in the footsteps of John Wood the Younger.

A ROOM WITH A VIEW
THE FIRST CRESCENT

A ROOM WITH A VIEW
THE FIRST CRESCENT

'Are we going to see the Crescent?' It is a question asked by almost every visitor to Bath, apparently unaware that the city has several crescents. The one they mean, of course, is the Royal Crescent, the first and greatest of them all. Even today, with its proportions marred by ruthless nineteenth-century window-lengthening, its stonework an odd patchwork where some houses have been cleaned and some not, its mixture of front-door colours, and the intrusion of cars parked along its length, it still works its awe-inspiring magic. Imagine how astonishing it must have been to eighteenth-century eyes, used to the enclosed spaces intended as backdrops to their colourful lives. Here nature was an important element in architecture where previously artifice had been all. The most puzzling thing about it is – how ever did John Wood the Younger come to think of it?

John Wood the Younger, although bearing his father's name, was a very different man. While Wood the Elder looked back to an idealized past, his son had his feet firmly in the present. Worthy, kindly and conscientious, he held the principle that 'no architect can form a convenient plan unless he ideally places himself in the situation of the person for whom he designs', a maxim he stated in his book of plans for cottages for labourers, published in 1781.

It is hard to imagine John Wood the Younger embarking on flights of fancy like those of his father. The kindest thing one can say about the external design of the Assembly Rooms, the only other major piece of work we know to be his, is that it is pedestrian. It is an early example of the shoebox style of architecture more usually associated with the 1960s. Could the man who designed this really have been inspired to produce something as revolutionary and original as the Royal Crescent? His supporters suggest a possible explanation. The recession of the 1750s brought Bath's boom, and with it work on the Circus, to a grinding halt. The first, west-facing segment of the Circus took twelve years to complete. It was not until the economy began to revive that John Wood the Younger was able to continue his building plans. It was during this time, it has been suggested, that he conceived the idea of a crescent similar in style to the unfinished Circus. But could an arc of buildings, facing *into* the hillside, really have inspired the glorious sweep of the Crescent? It does not seem very likely. A more plausible answer lies in the mystic dreams of his father.

John Wood the Elder was convinced that, in ancient times, there had been towers and temples in Bath dedicated to both the sun and the moon. Did he plan the Circus as a new temple to the sun? And if so, what about a temple to the moon? It would have to be a crescent. Was the Royal Crescent simply John Wood the Younger's realization of his father's dream?

RIGHT Columns stride majestically
around a semi-ellipse, its ends pulled in
so that the end houses face each other.

There is, however, a third possibility. The Grand Tour of Europe had become essential for any young man with pretensions to culture. While travelling he would collect works of art. In the eighteenth century, paintings of Arcadian scenes by artists such as Salvator Rosa, Nicolas Poussin and, above all, Claude Lorrain were particularly popular. It was these 'Claudian landscapes' that inspired the great English landscape gardeners such as Lancelot 'Capability' Brown. Perhaps the younger John Wood wandered across the fields to the west of the partly built Circus, his head full of his money troubles. Wood the father had left such big bequests to his favourite daughters that his widow and son were in financial difficulties. They were forced to carry on with speculative developments to borrow money and raise the necessary capital to pay the legacies. And then, as the younger Wood stopped to take a rest, he saw a Claudian landscape before his very eyes. The hills of Somerset loomed mistily in the distance, sheep and cattle grazed in the foreground. A glimpse of the incomplete south-west wing of the Circus recalled one of Claude's romantic ruins. Perhaps there was an alfresco party sitting under the trees, adding colour to the scene. Is this another answer to the conundrum? Did he, at this point, realize that he had found the ideal spot for a new development – that he could cash in on the new craze for 'prospects'? We will never know. Whatever the inspiration, John Wood the Younger gave to Bath one of the world's most famous buildings.

Work had resumed on the Circus as the economic situation improved. Brock Street, a street of plain but well-proportioned houses linking the Circus to the Crescent, had also been delayed by the slump, but work began again in 1763. Today the buildings are rather spoilt by the addition of some heavy nineteenth-century porches, and Wood's colour scheme of white woodwork and dark brown doors was abandoned long ago. The quiet calm of the street is almost certainly deliberate, so that nothing detracts from the great architectural showpieces at either end. If his father's ideas were the motivation, then Brock Street may have been seen as the Palladian equivalent of the avenues of stones that sometimes lead from one Neolithic monument to another.

RIGHT From the Gravel Walk, designed for sedan chairs, can be seen the back of the Circus, its higgledy-piggledy rear view in sharp contrast to its symmetrical front façade.

OPPOSITE Brock Street, its subdued Palladianism a relief from the glories of the Crescent and the Circus at each end, has suffered many changes over the years, especially to its door-cases. So far, no satisfactory explanation has been found for the charming Gothick porch at No. 16.

ABOVE In the nineteenth century the Royal Crescent, like so many other buildings, was subjected to window-lengthening and the removal of glazing bars.

OPPOSITE At No. 1, owned by Bath Preservation Trust, the windows have been restored.

What we do know is that Wood set up office in the house at the westernmost end of Brock Street, and advertised for prospective builders to come and view the land and the plans.

Deeds held in the Bath Record Office reveal more of the story. He took a lease on two fields, called Hayes Furlong and Hayes Lower Furlong, owned by Sir Benet Garrard. The lease was £30 per annum for two years but then rose to £220 per annum. Sir Benet was careful to lay down exactly what Wood could and could not do. He was allowed to put up a stone pillar to survey the land, but it was to be taken down if Sir Benet requested. Since it is no longer there, one may assume that he did. One option that was not taken up, sadly, was that for a model farmhouse and offices, to be built on the fields below the Crescent. A Wood farmhouse, based, perhaps, on his ideas for labourers' cottages, would have been an interesting addition to Bath's architectural treasures. It was also decreed that there would be a footway, a route for sedan chairs, running from behind the King's Circus and Brock Street to Queen Square. Today we call it the Gravel Walk. In the earliest leases there was going to be a reservoir but in the final lease, granted in 1771, it was stated that there would be no reservoir.

While Wood waited for the builders to apply to build in the Crescent, he surveyed the land and designed the façade. And what a façade! Bold, if somewhat severe, 114 Giant

Order Ionic columns stride majestically around a semi-ellipse with its ends pulled in so that the end houses face each other. Only the central house brings some relief from the relentless symmetry. No. 16, the best house in the Crescent, is distinguished by two pairs of double columns. Between the columns the central window is topped by a semicircular window, known as a lunette, or little moon. Is this simply an architectural device or could it also be a hint that this is what the Crescent is all about? Nikolaus Pevsner described the Crescent as splendid, magnificent, but not domestic, and there is truth in this. Like the moon, it has a chilly remoteness. In fairness to Wood, it must be said that some of this is due to window-lengthening and the removal of glazing bars. At No. 1, now owned by Bath Preservation Trust and run as a museum, the windows have been restored to their original length and the glazing bars reinstated. Palladian proportions were based around the size of the windows, and the whole structure has been affected by the nineteenth-century alterations which have pulled it in and given it a bleak, secretive look. If all the windows could be restored, the Crescent would appear to spread and look more benign.

Wood's brother-in-law, Thomas Brock (after whom Brock Street is named), built the first house in the Crescent, which acted as a model for the others. Leases stated that

ABOVE One of the world's most photographed views. The Crescent is glimpsed through this spectacular floral display – the pride of the Parks Department.

houses were to be no higher than Brock's and should have no cupola. As with many Georgian developments, the different builders who took up Wood's building leases constructed and fitted up the individual houses to their own designs – it was just the façade which had to fulfil the architect's plan. The backs of the houses were a complete hotchpotch, often built out of the cheaper (but more durable) ragstone, which was then hidden with render. Occasionally, when it was known that the backs would be open to public view, the developer would specify the rear design as well, usually insisting on Bath stone ashlar blocks. This is the case, for example, with the south side of Brock Street, which would be seen from the Gravel Walk.

From the outset it was plain that the Royal Crescent would be a stylish place to live. The houses were expensive. In 1771 the builder Michael Hemmings sold No. 7 to Elizabeth Tyndall for £1700, which included the fittings. The deeds relating to this house tell us what these were, and they make interesting reading. In the basement were a kitchen, wash-house, housekeeper's room, arched wine cellar and servants' privy 'neatly fitted up'. On the ground floor, the hall was paved with Portland stone dotted with black marble. Mrs Tyndall was unhappy with the window in the storeroom, which had to be altered. Shelves, drawers and cupboards had to be installed. The principal rooms had marble fireplaces

fitted with cast iron 'stoves', which today would be known as grates. The fireplace in the front parlour had black marble trimmings. Security was important to Mrs Tyndall. Locks were fitted on most doors, including those to the offices below stairs (she clearly did not trust the servants), and bolts were added to the sash windows. The privy in the garden was to be built to Elizabeth Tyndall's own specification. One wonders why she was so anxious about the plumbing. She was clearly having no truck with the not-so-newfangled but still accident-prone water closets.

Not all the houses in the Royal Crescent were intended as homes or lodgings. Mrs and Miss Rosco commissioned one as a school for young ladies. Unfortunately, there must have been some delays, for in January 1771 they advertised that they had taken a house in Brock Street until the house in the Crescent was ready. The annual fees were 5 guineas, and £30 for boarders. This included tea, washing and mending, as well as instruction in writing, accounts, French, English grammar and all kinds of needlework – everything, in fact, to turn untutored, naïve young girls into good wives, capable of keeping the accounts of a large house if married off to a wealthy suitor, or of exercising due economy if married to a humble, albeit well-connected, curate. We should not forget that Bath was not only a health resort and social centre, but was also famous as a marriage market.

ABOVE The return front at the western end of the Crescent.

Even before it was finished, the Crescent was a popular attraction. Prints of it were published while it was under construction. In them we can see not only the nascent Crescent but also some of the equipment that was used by eighteenth-century builders. One major piece of work was building the vaults beneath the footway, which served as storage space for everything from fresh water to dairy goods, wine and coal. All householders were promised free use of the open space in front of the Crescent, a right that is still jealously guarded today. The open space in question extended as far as the ha-ha, the sunken wall and ditch which kept the farm animals artistically in the middle distance without blocking the view. Today it serves to keep human animals and their canine friends from polluting the Crescent's hallowed turf.

In the forty years between the building of Queen Square and the building of the Royal Crescent, there had been major changes in Bath. Not only had it grown larger and more elegant, but it was also becoming genteel. Gone were the days when Lady Lechmere had gambled away up to £700 at one sitting, and Beau Nash had lived openly with his mistress, Juliana Popjoy. Gambling had long been controlled by Act of Parliament, so that it was an offence to lose more than £10. Nash had poured scorn on the moralists but in 1777 Captain Wade was forced to resign from his post as Master of Ceremonies when he was accused of seducing a lady. Where courtesans such as Lady Townshend and Kitty Edwin had once entranced fashionable society with their scandalous behaviour, now parties of sedate clergymen felt it safe to take their ease. Yet even in this atmosphere, scandal and intrigue had a way of breaking through the polite veneer.

The Duke of York, George III's son and the 'Grand Old Duke of York' of the nursery rhyme, stayed in the Royal Crescent – at No. 1 and No. 16 – in 1796. Despite the rhyme's insinuations of incompetence, he brought much-needed reforms to the Army. But his character was besmirched when, in 1809, he was accused, together with his mistress, Mary Anne Clarke, of selling commissions. The Princesse de Lamballe is also believed to have stayed at No. 1, in 1786. Using a pseudonym, this friend of Marie Antoinette seems to have been on a secret mission to persuade the Government not to give shelter to French dissidents such as Marat. Six years later the French Revolution was brought uncomfortably close to her former neighbours when they opened their papers to read that she had been hacked to pieces and her head stuck on a pike. The Royal Crescent also has a fictional connection with the French Revolution in the person of the Scarlet Pimpernel, who, according to Baroness Orczy, lived at No. 15.

LEFT The Royal Crescent in winter, its uncompromising symmetry clearly revealed. Only the central house, No. 16, with its double columns and lunette over the central window, offers any variation.

Another French resident was the unfortunate Vicomte Jean Du Barré, brother-in-law (and former lover) of Madame Du Barré, the notorious mistress of Louis XV of France. Du Barré, with his Irish friend Count Rice, ran a gambling den at No. 8. Having (illegally) won a substantial sum from Colonel Champion, who lived at No. 29, Du Barré and Rice fell out over the division of the winnings, and fought a duel on Claverton Down, south of the city, in which Du Barré was killed.

Hanging was the ultimate fate of Dr Dodd, who preached the first sermon at Margaret's Chapel in Brock Street, the proprietary chapel for the Crescent. A charismatic preacher, much admired by women for his good looks, he was convicted of forging a bond. Since the money had immediately been repaid, the jury urged clemency – but in vain. Despite a vigorous campaign by his friends, including Dr Johnson and Lord Chesterfield (the man against whose name the bond had been forged), he went to the gallows.

Christopher Anstey, who lived at No. 4, managed to get his name in the papers for a different reason. The son of a Cambridgeshire rector, and a country gentleman, he might easily be forgotten were it not for his highly developed sense of the absurd. This had cost him his Master's degree at Cambridge, when he poked fun at the requirement to make a speech in Latin. In 1766, after a visit to Bath, he published *The New Bath Guide* or the *Memoirs of the B-R-D Family* in a series of *Poetical Episodes*. It tells the adventures of Simkin Blunderhead, a countrified gentleman who comes to Bath with his family to take the waters. Today it is of interest to us for what it tells us about Bath rather than for its wit, but in 1766 society was enchanted. Horace Walpole, writing to his friend George Montagu, declared: 'What pleasure you have to come! There is a new thing published that will make you bepiss your cheeks with laughing. It is called The New Bath Guide . . . so much wit, so much humour, fun and poetry, so much originality, never met together before.' All would have been well if Anstey had left it there, but unfortunately he did not. He began to take himself seriously. He became one of the Miller coterie, a group of mainly second-rate poets who enjoyed the hospitality of Sir John and Lady Miller at their house at Batheaston. Horace Walpole lampooned them mercilessly, and in 1774 an anonymous article in a London paper savaged not only the Millers, but also Anstey himself. Anstey rose to the bait. Convinced it was an Anglican clergyman who was responsible, he published a poem called *The Priest Dissected*. It was heavy-handed, confused, and sounds almost like a parody itself, although it was deadly serious. He also had to refute rumours that he was the author of a satirical poem attacking the King. After all this one would have thought that Anstey would have learnt his lesson,

RIGHT The northern end of Margaret's Buildings, well known to bibliophiles for its second-hand and antiquarian bookshops.

but in 1776 he wrote a another comic poem, poking fun at a post-election ball held at the Upper Rooms. It was not very amusing, but is noteworthy to us not only for its descriptions of clothes – especially women's underwear – but also for the occasional coarseness of its language. To the relief of his fellow residents in the Crescent, this brief foray into the Grub Street press was enough for Anstey. He began to shun the limelight, eventually sinking into a quiet retirement, though he could not resist dropping a literary bombshell once in a while.

However, Anstey's life-story was a mild affair compared to that of the man parodied in *The New Bath Guide* as Captain Cormorant. This was Philip Thicknesse, possibly one of the most unpleasant people ever to walk Bath's streets. Thicknesse was famous for being appallingly rude. He had been dismissed from the Army not only for his outbursts of temper, but also for his ability to pursue a feud. On the death of his first wife through diphtheria, he wrote to his mother-in-law to tell her that although her daughter and grandchildren were dead and he was almost dead, there was one bright light on the horizon – he would not have to have anything to do with her again. His son George, by his second wife Elizabeth, inherited a title. Thicknesse – who had no title and dearly wanted one – was furious. He waited till after his death to be revenged upon George, who found the following codicil in his father's will: 'I leave my right hand, to be cut off after my death, to my son, Lord Audley, and I desire it may be sent to him in hopes that such a sight may remind him of his duty to God, after having for so long abandoned the duty he owed his father who once affectionately loved him.' Anstey also suffered at Thicknesse's hands, when the latter produced *The New Prose Bath Guide* in 1778 as a riposte to Anstey's book.

The neighbours must have been far from delighted when Thicknesse and his third wife, Ann Ford, moved into 9 Royal Crescent. Thomas Gainsborough was irritated to find that Thicknesse told everyone that it was he who had spotted the young painter's talent and persuaded him to come to Bath. Nevertheless the good-natured artist painted an extraordinary and striking picture of Ann Ford. Sitting with crossed legs, the swell of which can clearly be seen beneath her oyster-coloured silk dress, she leans on one elbow, her face wearing a defiant smile. Her pose breaks all the rules for decorous young ladies. No wonder that Mrs Mary Delany declared: 'I should be very sorry to have anyone I loved set forth in such a manner.' No wonder,

either, that the unconventional Ann Ford should have loved it and ordered a matching one to be done of her husband. Unfortunately, Gainsborough found Philip Thicknesse an uncongenial subject. He started work on the painting but soon gave up. The Thicknesses demanded the picture, on the grounds that Ann Ford had given the viola da gamba in her portrait to the music-loving Gainsborough in payment. In vain did the artist protest that he had paid for the instrument. Eventually, he handed over the painting as it stood – just barely sketched out. From then on Thicknesse sniped relentlessly at Gainsborough, and even more so at Gainsborough's wife, for whom he had developed an implacable hatred. It is possible that this was a contributory factor in Gainsborough's decision to leave Bath. One artist who found no trouble in drawing Thicknesse was the caricaturist James Gillray. He portrayed him as Lieutenant Governor Gallstones, sitting on a lavatory and dipping his pen in bile. The Royal Crescent's residents must have heaved a sigh of relief when he sold his house there and moved to Lansdown.

The story which really had the gossips' tongues wagging was that of Elizabeth Linley's elopement with Richard Sheridan. The Linley family, known as 'the nest of nightingales' because of their musicianship, were living at 11 Royal Crescent in 1772. Gainsborough painted portraits of several of them. In particular, Elizabeth, a timeless beauty, was something of a muse for him. In one of his portraits, her dark hair floats like a cloud around her face, which wears an enigmatic expression. Yet Gainsborough's painting of her father, Thomas Linley, is even more striking. This is a cruel portrait – there is no flattery here. Everything we know about this calculating, materialistic man is evident in this painting. He saw his children as an investment, Elizabeth being the jewel in the crown. Naturally he was dismayed when he found she had fallen in love with an impecunious young Irish playwright called Richard Sheridan. The playwright's father was equally upset – he had better plans for Richard than marriage to a singer. The most famous part of their love affair, the elopement on 18 March 1772, appears to have come about more as an act of chivalry than as the result of overwhelming passion. Elizabeth, pursued by unwanted suitors and tired of singing in public, arranged with Richard's sister Betsy Sheridan to escape to France with Richard as an escort. While there, Richard and Elizabeth may have gone through a form of marriage before she retreated to a convent. Eventually, after many

vicissitudes, the parents gave in and Elizabeth and Richard were married. But the story did not have a happy ending. Richard proved unfaithful to Elizabeth, who died at the age of thirty-eight, a neglected wife.

Somewhat ironically, the woman who captured Sheridan's fickle heart after he tired of Elizabeth Linley came as a guest to a house only a stone's throw away, in Marlborough Buildings. Unlike the Crescent, the Buildings are not the work of a single architect. The three central houses bear all the hallmarks of Thomas Baldwin, the City Surveyor who also built the Guildhall, and they may well be earlier than the other houses. Also earlier is the Marlborough Tavern at the top of the row. This was probably built for tired chairmen who had carried overweight invalids up to the Crescent and now faced a long journey back to the chair rank. By 1790 the rest of the terrace was complete and the name of the street was changed from Milk Street to Marlborough Buildings. Almost certainly the name comes from the brook which ran in the valley behind the houses. This was known as the Muddlebrook; to our ears this may sound nothing like Marlborough, but in the eighteenth century both Muddlebrook and Marlborough were pronounced Marlbrook.

In 1791 the Duke of Devonshire and his beautiful wife, Georgiana, took two houses in Marlborough Buildings, one for themselves and one for their son, the Marquis of Hartington. The Duchess was in terror that her sickly son might contract smallpox, and no one could be admitted to his house unless they were known to be free of the disease. With the Duchess came her sister, Lady Harriet Duncannon. She was in a poor state of health, suffering from a mysterious illness that may have been depression, but may equally have resulted from a failed suicide attempt. She was

trapped in a desperately unhappy marriage and involved in an affair with a Whig politician and playwright – none other than Richard Brinsley Sheridan.

Georgiana also had her anxieties. Fanny Burney was living in Bath at the time and, although she was determined to have nothing to do with this scandalous family whose politics she totally opposed, was won over by Georgiana's charm. Fanny, however, was no fool. 'She appeared to me not happy,' she wrote of the Duchess. 'I thought she looked oppressed within – though there is a native cheerfulness about her which I fancy scarce ever deserts her.' What no one at the time realized, except Georgiana herself, was that the Duchess was pregnant by her lover, Charles Grey. It was to become a scandal that shook the Cavendish family to its foundations.

West of Marlborough Buildings lay the Bath Commons. These were controlled by the Freemen of Bath, who during the late Georgian period made several attempts to build on this undeveloped farmland. Unluckily for the Freemen, Sir Nicholas Hyde, the Recorder of Bath in 1619, had declared that the fields should never be built on. This meant that, as fast as the Freemen produced plans, the Corporation turned them down. In 1827, they produced an idea for an estate which would have stretched over both Middle and High Commons. It bore remarkable similarities to Pittville, the estate which had been built in Bath's rival spa, Cheltenham, just a few years earlier. There would have been thirty-two villas on Middle Common, and twenty-seven on High Common. It would have been an interesting addition to Bath's architectural scene, but would have deprived the city of one of its finest open spaces. Fortunately the Corporation rejected the plans, declaring that the fields had been open 'from time immemorial'. The Freemen abandoned their ideas for development but some concerned citizens met to discuss a plan for creating 'ornamental plantations, walks and rides'. The city had long had pleasure gardens, such as Spring Gardens, Sydney Gardens and the ill-fated Grosvenor Gardens, on the London Road, plagued by mists and damp from the River Avon. These charged for admission, and were, in their own way, the forerunners of amusement parks. They were certainly not educational and by 1829 all had either closed or were run down. There was a movement afoot in Europe to build promenades and public gardens and there was another more pressing need for an up-to-date attraction: Bath was suffering one of its periodic slumps in tourism.

RIGHT High Common, where in the early nineteenth century the Freemen of Bath planned an estate in the style of Pittville, in Cheltenham. The remains of a Roman villa were found on the allotments at the rear of Marlborough Buildings, which can be seen in the distance.

ABOVE The face of the eighteen-year-old Victoria on the obelisk in the Royal Victoria Park. Someone has given her red lips – in the 1870s the obelisk was daubed with red paint.

The first area to be considered was that known as Crescent Fields, the farmland which lay below the Crescent itself. However, the reformers soon switched their attention to the Bath Commons. These were criss-crossed by footpaths and contained several small quarries. In 1829, various plans to beautify the area were put forward. One scheme proposed by a Mr Hobson included zoological and botanical gardens on High Common, with grottoes, conservatories and refreshment booths in the style of temples. It was very like Sydney Gardens and completely ignored the latest trends in garden design. However, the architect Edward Davis, a student of Sir John Soane, put forward plans which included a carriage drive on High Common, an ornamental drive and lodge houses on Middle Common, and gardens on Crescent Fields. The first question was whether Lady Rivers Gay, the landowner, would allow a carriage drive and gardens on Crescent Fields. She willingly granted the lease, so the first hurdle was cleared. It was to be over forty years, however, before the park assumed the shape it is today.

Grandiose gates, designed by Edward Davis in a very Soanian style, were erected as fitting entrances to the park. The nearby farmhouse was Gothicized in the *cottage ornée* style advocated by the garden expert J.C. Loudon. Although the rebuilding of the cottage is usually ascribed to Davis, the

Bath Chronicle reported in 1831 that it was the work of G.P. Manners. Prettified as it was, it was still a working farmhouse, and the greater part of what is now the park was still part of the farm. The park consisted of a belt of ornamental trees around the central fields. The opening of this park in 1830 was attended by the eleven-year-old Princess Victoria, who was staying in Bath at the time, and she agreed that it should henceforth be known as the Royal Victoria Park.

There is an apocryphal story concerning Princess Victoria's visit. It is frequently said that, while driving through the park, she overheard a small boy making rude comments about her legs. She was so offended that she thereafter hated Bath, so much so that she refused to visit it again. When, in later life, she passed through on the train, she pulled down the blinds as she travelled through Bath Spa station. All of this is nonsense. In later years she recalled her visit to Bath with affection, saying that the most memorable event for her had been a ride in a sedan chair (which must have been a blow for all the dignitaries that she had met – but she was only eleven). And when she travelled through by train, far from pulling down the blinds, she stood at the window and waved to the crowds.

In tribute to the Princess, the park committee built the obelisk which stands just inside the main gates to the park.

ABOVE One of the Coad stone lions at the entrance to the park gazes at a hot air balloon.

PAGES 130–131
SCENES FROM THE PARK
CLOCKWISE FROM LEFT
Royal Victoria Park – Bath's biggest park; a magnolia in the Botanical Gardens; the ladies' bowling team; the pavilion and doves in the Botanical Gardens.

The foundation stone was laid in October 1837 to commemorate her eighteenth birthday. By the time it was complete, Victoria was Queen. Important events in her reign were commemorated on the obelisk. Today, a tour twice around it serves as a brief summary of the Victorian era.

Initially, visitors to the park had to pay a small entrance fee. Those wishing to ride through had to become subscribers. However, this did not stop vandalism, which was a problem right from the start. In 1835, for example, the paper reported that 'some loathsomely brutal rascals' had damaged and torn down the young trees. This arboreal attack took on a political dimension when the Radicals accused the Tories of employing the vandals, although what political advantage they thought they would gain by pulling up trees is unclear. The staunchly right-wing *Bath Chronicle* was outraged. 'There are among the radicals of Bath, men whom we think capable of much that is bad and malicious, but it really would never have entered into our minds to accuse any one among them of being so utterly lost to all sense of manliness and rectitude, as to find it in his heart to make so wanton and so totally groundless a charge as this,' thundered the editor. He concluded that such degraded people were more to be pitied than despised.

When Bath Corporation finally acquired the park in 1879, animals were still grazing on large parts of it. Various developments were proposed: some, like the bandstand, were realized, and some, like Winter Gardens based on the Crystal Palace, were not. Today the park is an important feature of the city's life. As well as flower beds and botanical gardens, it offers golf courses, tennis courts and a children's play area. Events such as the Spring Flower Show and the Easter Funfair take place in its grounds. The Bath International Music Festival begins with an evening of free entertainment on the Crescent Fields, culminating in a firework display. Above all, the park is somewhere for residents and tourists alike to relax and enjoy themselves. Few, however, will be aware that the paths they walk on follow the line of footpaths that crossed it centuries ago, and that one of its trees, a gnarled old hawthorn, is a remnant of the hedges which stood here long before the two John Woods had dreamed of the Circus or the Crescent.

The Commons acted as a green belt, limiting the westward expansion of the city. Developers turned instead to the slopes above the Royal Crescent. North of the Crescent, beyond the road then known as Cottle's Lane, was an orchard and gardens enjoyed by the early residents of the Crescent. However, in 1790, Sir Peter Rivers Gay, the landowner, granted a lease to two local builders, who hired the architect John Palmer to design a square. Christopher Anstey, one of the affected residents, wrote an angry poem

which pointed out that tenants were already hard to come by and the best development would be to build a madhouse or enlarge the jail. The protest was in vain. By 1794 Palmer's square, to be known as St James's Square, was more or less complete. It has an unusual design, with the streets entering it diagonally at the corners. The site seems to have given Palmer some problems, for he made an error in the southern range, placing the central feature off-centre. The side ranges also step rather awkwardly up the hill.

One of the houses on the eastern range is the proud possessor of two of the bronze plaques that can be seen on various Bath buildings. Most were put up during the early twentieth century at the instigation of the energetic alderman Thomas Sturge Cotterell. Sadly, the siting and wording of many plaques has proved, in the light of later research, to be somewhat unreliable, and these two are no exception. The first says that the essayist and poet Walter Savage Landor lived here: this is true, but he also lived in several other houses in St James's Square (not all at once). The second says that Charles Dickens dwelt here. In fact Dickens did not even spend a night here, although he did dine with Landor on several occasions, once accompanied by the American poet Longfellow. Another visitor was Thomas Carlyle. Today St James's Square is rather a quiet backwater – it is hard to imagine these literary giants knocking on the door of one of its houses.

East of St James's Square lies Portland Place. This is a little earlier than St James's Square, dating from around 1787, and was built on an orchard belonging to George Duperre, perfumier in Wade's Passage. The developer was John Hensley, originally a coachbuilder in Broad Street, and an astute businessman. His policy of buying up ground rents meant that by the time he died in 1803 he was an extremely rich man. Many of the houses in Portland Place were lodging houses, but among the long-term residents was Captain Matthews, who had been Sheridan's rival for the hand of Elizabeth Linley.

In 1817 a proprietary chapel for Portland Place was built at the bottom of Harley Street. A rather attractive building in a severe but elegant Greek Revival style, it was to have a chequered history. By 1832 it had become a Roman Catholic chapel, but in 1841 it came back into the hands of the Church of England, and was known as St Austin's. In 1848 it struck an early blow for sexual equality by having a female organist, Eliza Sherborne, and a sextoness, Hester Cooper. In 1870, work started on a new church, St Andrew's, behind the Royal Crescent, almost opposite the chapel. Although an impressive building in its own right, it was totally out of place, with its spire poking up like a finger above the Royal Crescent. In April 1942 it was, as Pevsner cruelly but accurately puts it, 'happily bombed'. The large green at the

back of the Royal Crescent marks its site. Harley Street Chapel was also destroyed in the air raids of that time, and a block of flats called Phoenix House later rose from the ashes.

There was also development south of Crescent Fields, down towards the river. In 1766 lodgings were advertised at the first new-built house in King Street (later New King Street) and in 1767 it is recorded that a new-built house in Charles Street had been burnt down. These houses were miniature versions of the houses built for Bath's wealthy visitors; it is possible to view one by visiting 19 New King Street, which now houses the Herschel Museum. Like Walter Savage Landor, William Herschel seemed constantly to be moving house, but it is with this building and 5 Rivers Street that he is most associated.

Herschel came to Bath from Hanover, a German state famous for its musicians. It was, for example, a Hanoverian band which played in the park. Herschel arrived in 1766, and took lodgings in Bell Lane before moving on to Beaufort Square. His move to a more fashionable address was doubtless due to his appointment as organist at the Octagon Chapel, the proprietary chapel for Milsom Street. This was in addition to playing the oboe in Thomas Linley's Pump Room orchestra. His brother Alexander came over to join

him, and then, on a visit home in 1772, William discovered that his sister Caroline was being used as little better than a drudge by her parents. Furious, he whisked her over to Bath where, in addition to keeping house for her two brothers at 7 King Street, she was persuaded to sing, and became a part of the musical ensemble. Soon she found that she was also to join another team. The brothers had developed a strong interest in astronomy, and as telescopes were constructed the house came to resemble a workshop, full of mirrors and lenses. They shared the house with another family and friction seems to have arisen, as a result of which they moved out to a house on the London Road. But they were soon back in New King Street, at No. 19. Two years later they moved again, to Rivers Street. Here, one night when Herschel was standing in the street observing the moon through a telescope, a passer-by, William Watson, asked him if he could have a look. This was a fortunate meeting, for Watson was an influential member of the Royal Society.

After four years at Rivers Street, the Herschels returned to 19 New King Street. It was here, while scanning the skies, that William Herschel observed an object which he did not recognize. At first he thought it was a comet, but astronomers soon realized that he had discovered a

previously unknown planet. Herschel christened it 'Georgius Sidus', in honour of George III, who was a keen amateur astronomer. However, European astronomers preferred Uranus, the name by which it is universally known today.

As the eighteenth century drew to a close, another crescent was started down by the river. This was Norfolk Crescent, now once again a fashionable area after having fallen on hard times when this part of the city became rather industrial. Work on Norfolk Crescent, as on nearby Green Park Buildings, progressed in fits and starts. Twenty years after work had begun, Norfolk Crescent was still incomplete. It was only after the Napoleonic threat had receded that it was finished. Like Green Park, it probably suffered from what Jane Austen referred to darkly as 'the damps', but, as with Nelson Place and Nile Street, its name is a memorial to one of Bath's famous residents, Horatio Nelson.

Let us now turn to an area of Bath well known to the Romans – the triangle that today is bordered by Walcot Street, the Paragon and Broad Street.

STREET OF STRANGERS

WHERE WEALTH AND POVERTY MET

STREET OF STRANGERS

WHERE WEALTH AND POVERTY MET

ABOVE AND OPPOSITE
What was once the cattle market
is now the busy Saturday
antiques market.

PAGES 136–137
A flavour of Walcot Street.

Walcot Street today is a lively, colourful place, which, with its variety of inhabitants and assortment of businesses and craft shops, has forged a unique identity. This expresses itself once a year during the Bath Festival Fringe, when the street celebrates Walcot Nation Day. In a way, this modern identity epitomizes its history – a mixture of cultures and classes, trades and professions, rich and poor.

Walcot Street runs parallel to a Roman road which was slightly nearer the river. Archaeological excavations indicate that the area was probably not much different from the way it is today. There were no great villas. Instead there was a mixture of shops, workshops and homes. An exciting archaeological discovery of recent years is the body of a potter, who seems to have originated in Syria or Egypt. He probably came to Britain attracted by commercial possibilities in the expanding Roman Empire. His presence reminds us how varied the peoples of the Empire were; our multicultural society would not have been strange to the people of Aquae Sulis. Even after the Roman army left Britain and many local people withdrew within the defensive rampart of the inner city, members of this diverse community continued to live outside the wall. When the Saxons eventually arrived, they considered these people to be strangers. Their word for strangers was *welisc* or *wealh*, from which we get the names Wales, Cornwall and Walcot – the place of strangers.

At some time in the Saxon period, Walcot Street was moved slightly higher up the hillside. Why this was done is not known; perhaps it was as a result of rising river levels or of a landslip which buried the Roman buildings that have recently been rediscovered by Bath Archaeological Trust. Other changes also occurred. Over the centuries the street became a garden suburb of Bath. Sizeable houses overlooked the river, with gardens stretching down to its banks. A seventeenth-century painting of one of them, Ladymead House, survives in Bath's Victoria Art Gallery. A weaving community gathered around the church of St Michael, which stood just outside the city wall, while a small village grew up around the ancient church of St Swithin, at the other end of Walcot Street. In the eighteenth century, as Bath began to flourish, Walcot gradually resumed its former working-class character. The cattle market with its associated trades moved into the area. Rows of back-to-back houses were squeezed into the gaps between buildings, on the site of once-tranquil gardens. 'Sorry I am to say,' wrote John Wood, 'that so charming a tract of land should be sacrificed to ancient and modern ignorance, but so it is. For instead of finding it covered with habitations for the chief citizens, it is filled, for the most part, with hovels for the refuse of the people.' Inns, pubs and alehouses sprang up along the street's length. To the confusion of later

LEFT AND RIGHT Statues, old clocks, bugles, fur coats and a host of other items can be purchased in the shops, markets and reclamation stores of Walcot Street.

OPPOSITE, CLOCKWISE FROM TOP LEFT A sewing machine hangs where once was the sign of the New Inn, just one of Walcot Street's many pubs; there's even a home for an old oilcan; a glass-beaded curtain in one of the shops.

historians, what is now one street was divided into three sections – Walcot Street, Ladymead and Cornwell Buildings. Perhaps the best way to explore its history is to step inside a virtual time machine and take an imaginary journey along its length.

We should begin where the old Northgate stood. This was torn down in 1755 because it impeded the flow of traffic into the city. Just outside the Northgate stood a clutch of coaching inns ready to catch passing trade as a constant stream of visitors arrived in the city. On the right were the Three Cups, the Three Horseshoes, the Boat (later renamed the Unicorn when the old Unicorn was pulled down to make way for the new Guildhall) and the Packhorse. On the other side of the street, where the Central Post Office now stands, was the Castle, sometimes known as the Castle and Ball. Many coaching inns were drastically reduced in size when the railway came in 1840, but the Castle was not one of them. As late as 1923 there were plans to rebuild it as a hotel, on the lines of the Grand Pump Room Hotel in Stall Street or the Empire in the Orange Grove. However, it was decided to put the Central Post Office there instead. The design of the post office is remarkably similar to that of the proposed hotel, and its yard is the same shape as the old inn yard. While the other inns have vanished completely, the Castle has at least left its mark on this part of Bath.

In front of us is the church of St Michael, also known as St Michael Without, because it is without (or outside) the city wall. It stands on a very ancient site. We know that there have been at least three churches here, but archaeologists now suggest that there may have been four, the earliest of them dating from Saxon or even late Roman times. Of the three we can be sure about, the earliest dated from the thirteenth century and was a typical small English parish church, with a nave, chancel and tower. It managed to sit across the rather cramped site so that it was aligned in the approved fashion, with the altar at the east end. Originally it was roofed in lead, but in 1581 the Council, needing lead to repair the pipes bringing water into the city, stripped it from the church roof and replaced it with stone tiles. This is not the best way to preserve an ancient building, and by 1730 it was in very poor shape. John Wood, who was building Queen Square at the time, offered to rebuild the church, on condition that he could retain the old materials for his own use and have pews set aside for the residents of Queen Square. As we have already seen, John Wood was not the most tactful of men, and he managed to upset the parish council. They refused his offer and turned instead to the local architect John Harvey. They would have done better to swallow their pride and stick with Wood. Harvey designed a church which seems to have been of quite astonishing ugliness. John Wood, in his

LEFT The spire of St Michael's Without. This church, which is at least the third on the site, was designed in the 1830s by the City Architect, G.P. Manners.

RIGHT Christmas lights in Broad Street. St Michael's is at the bottom of the hill, with the Abbey tower in the distance.

Description of Bath, said it was so ugly that workmen had to cover a horse's head to persuade it to go past. He was hardly an impartial critic, but his opinion is borne out by later writers, including Pierce Egan who, in 1819, said 'it was an annoyance to admirers of architecture in Bath'. Eventually, in 1835, the parish council called in G.P. Manners, the City Architect, who designed the church which now occupies the site, based on the Early English style of Salisbury Cathedral.

As our time machine moved up the street, we would be astonished at the number of inns and beerhouses there were, particularly in the nineteenth century. Many were short-lived. The New Inn was one such. It was opened in 1848 by a shoemaker to augment his income, but he drank the profits (such as they were) and, faced with ruin, cut his own throat. Others were more successful. The George had a cockpit – in the early eighteenth century a sure sign that gentry stayed there. By the early nineteenth century cock-fighting was banned, and the inn's owners looked for other attractions to replace it, such as Drake's Menagerie, with an elephant, hyenas, bears and porpoises. The George's business, like that of other inns, was hit badly by the coming of the railway. Eventually parts of the inn were sold off and it dwindled to a shadow of its former self. Today it has vanished completely, but you can still find lodgings there, for the new YMCA block stands on the site.

A similar fate befell the Pelican. Built by 1757, it had stabling for forty horses and was Walcot Street's most prestigious inn. A plaque on its wall claimed that Dr Samuel Johnson stayed there but, although his ever-present one-man fan club, James Boswell, did have lodgings there, the doctor actually stayed with his friends the Thrales on South Parade. Doubtless the Great Man, escaping from the anxious administrations of Hettie Thrale and her friend Fanny Burney, was happy to sit with Boswell in the bar and down a bottle of wine or two. Sixty years later, as Georgette Heyer describes in her novel *Lady of Quality*, the Pelican was still respectable but no longer frequented by fashionable society. Its food was described as being adequate but plain. Part of the Pelican was renamed the Three Cups when Thomas Smith moved there from the old Three Cups, on Northgate Street, in 1849, and the remainder became shops and houses. Eventually, in the 1960s, it was demolished.

The loss of Walcot Street's pubs has been a gradual process. Some, such as the Jolly Sailor, the Red Lion, and the Carpenter's Arms, only had a fleeting existence. Others, like the Catherine Wheel, the Hand and Shears, the Bladud's Head and the Beehive Inn had a long (and sometimes dishonourable) history. Today only the Bell survives. It dates back at least as far as 1728. In the eighteenth century it was a hive of activity, as lumbering carts, wagons and 'caravans' (the Georgian equivalent of the modern white delivery van) left from its stable yard. Those in charge of these vehicles were not noted for their sobriety. Accidents involving them were frequent, and drunken driving and racing other carts were regular occurrences. Sometimes the driver simply fell in a drunken stupor from his seat. Today the Bell is equally colourful, although in a different way. It is the headquarters of the Bath Fringe Festival, live bands play there and it has a formidable array of real ales and a clientele of all ages, classes and nationalities.

However, the Bell has recently been joined by an open-plan bar, the Ha! Ha! Bar, in the unlikely surroundings of the old tram shed. The first tramlines in Bath were laid in Walcot Street in 1880, for horse trams. By 1900 a plan to introduce electric trams was well under way, and the power station was built on part of the old Walcot Foundry site at the back of the Beehive Inn. Next door was an old malthouse and its outhouses. This plot was purchased to build a tram shed for eight cars. The cavernous building was constructed of brick, with white tiles on the south side. Almost certainly these were intended to deflect heat from the interior of the shed,

cutting down on the fire risk. While this was doubtless effective technically, it gave the structure a rather lavatorial appearance. After trams gave way to buses in 1939, the tram shed went through a variety of uses. It even survived the architectural carnage of the 1960s, when many perfectly good Georgian buildings were pulled down. Now, after years of near dereliction, it has sprung to life with shops, penthouse flats and the aforementioned bar. Somewhat surprisingly, it works rather well, its open front adapting happily to twenty-first-century glass architecture, but its new use would doubtless surprise the board of the Bath and District Light Railway Company, who first built it.

In our time machine, we might be regretting that we cannot take part in every aspect of the street's life but we should be glad that all our senses are not in play. The smell of parts of Walcot Street would have been eye-watering. In the nineteenth century there were not only breweries and malthouses but also stable yards with their steaming mounds of horse manure. Added to that were the smoke and fumes from the foundry and, on market days, the heady scent of frightened animals. The first charter for a market was granted in 1317, and although the main food market was within the city walls, the cattle, sheep, pig and corn market was in Walcot Street. Associated with it were slaughter-houses, tripe-boilers and tanneries – all fairly pungent trades. On market days the street was filled with sheep pens. At times animals would succeed in escaping, causing havoc as they dashed through the streets. The first cornmarket hall was built in the early nineteenth century, and remodelled about eighty years later. The 1813 *Bath Guidebook* describes it as having secure granaries for safely lodging unsold grain, and vaults beneath (still visible today) which were 'well-calculated for wholesome slaughter-houses'. In 1855 the Corporation, concerned about all the wheeling and dealing that was carried on in Walcot Street's pubs, opened a new cornmarket hall and then went off to a celebratory lunch – in another Walcot Street pub, the Bladud's Head.

Someone else concerned about the amount of drinking was Miss Elizabeth Landon. In 1864 she paid for a horse trough and drinking fountain, which can still seen at the widest point of Walcot Street. Designed by Major Davis, the City Engineer, it was 'composed of specimens from all the various building stones found in the immediate neighbourhood', to which was added granite and white marble. Although the horses used the trough, most of the farmers continued to prefer real ale to Adam's ale. Today, looking rather dejected, the horse trough serves as a flower bed, but plans are afoot to restore it. The 1885 Ordnance Survey map suggests that it was the site of the Carn Well, after which Cornwell Buildings is named and whose waters were supposed to be effective in curing eye disorders. John Wood, however, recorded that the well had disappeared in road widening, and his description suggests that it was further up Walcot Street, nearer the Bell.

Perhaps the strangest alteration we would see is the change in fortune of the once countrified Ladymead House. In 1805 it became a penitentiary where 'forty six females of fallen reputations should find shelter, advice and encouragement to return to the paths of virtue'. It was, in other words, a place where prostitutes, many of whom had been thrown on to the streets after being ill-treated, seduced or even raped while in service, were trained in domestic skills so that they could be returned to exactly the same employment that had started them on the downward path. Small wonder that several escaped, while others were expelled for being disorderly. In 1816 a lock hospital was added where the unhappy women who had contracted

sexually transmitted diseases were treated. As the name suggests, they had little choice in the matter, being imprisoned in the ward. After nine years, the hospital was converted to a chapel that could seat three hundred, in addition to the 'penitents'. Today the house provides shelter for a very different kind of 'female' – retired ladies.

One of the principal benefactors of the penitentiary was Mr Parish, who was also involved with the Bath and Bathforum Free School next to Ladymead House. Founded in 1810, it was non-denominational and open to all poor children. It was associated with a pin manufactory, which was intended to keep idle young hands from getting into mischief. Later the manufactory moved to Morford Street on Lansdown, because the officials were concerned about the low characters that the children saw on their way through Walcot Street. Pin-making was an important local industry, for the elaborate dresses of the eighteenth and nineteenth centuries required masses of them. Later on, far grander premises were built for Walcot schools, first of all near the Paragon and then at the top end of Walcot Street. This latter school is now part of the St Swithin's Yard development,

RIGHT Eventually Walcot Street turns into London Street, more or less on the line of the Roman road that led eastwards out of Aquae Sulis.

ABOVE The Hat and Feather is another lively pub at the far end of Walcot Street.

ABOVE RIGHT The archangel St Michael, by Wallace Gill, balletically slays the devil on St Michael's church house, one of Bath's rare examples of Art Nouveau. The building is now an office.

named after the patron saint of Walcot parish church, which stands at the far end of the street with its entrance in the Paragon. It was here, where the two streets met, that the rough and tumble of Walcot Street rubbed shoulders with the quiet elegance and wealth of the Paragon. It was not always a happy meeting. Early one Sunday morning in 1842, for example, one Edward Thomas tumbled out of the White Horse Cellar, a pub that stood opposite the church, in a state of 'beastly intoxication'. He proceeded to behave towards shocked churchgoers in such 'an insolent and disgraceful manner' that he was promptly arrested.

Walcot church was founded over a thousand years ago by Bath's own saint, St Alphege. Its dedication to St Swithin, the patron saint of Winchester, was probably a political move. Swithin had been a loyal servant of the kings of Wessex, as was Dunstan, Archbishop of Canterbury when Alphege was founding Walcot church. This early building was just a small village church, remnants of which are preserved in the present crypt. It seems to have survived until the eighteenth century, although it was probably much altered over the years. With the expansion of Bath, it was felt that the church should be rebuilt. John Wood the Elder submitted plans which were rejected in favour of plans by a churchwarden, Robert Smith. Sometimes described as a rebuilding, it appears to have been more of a remodelling. It

was not until 1774 that a totally new church was begun to a plan by John Palmer. This was described as a 'neat modern structure'. Its rather unusual tower and steeple were added in 1790. The church contains monuments from the old church, including one to Thomas and Mary Fry, the children of the Rector of Walcot in 1683, both of whom died of smallpox.

This sad memorial brings the past sharply into focus, for it is people, their lives and their deaths, their joys and their sadness, which make a community. So let us, for a moment, travel back once again in our time machine and watch some of the people who have lived in, worked in or just visited Walcot Street. As we go back into the distant past, the figures become shadowy – we can only guess at their lives. In the Roman street, our Middle Eastern potter is working alongside other craftsmen: glass-makers, ironsmiths, jewellers, tile-makers, all supplying goods for the bustling town of Aquae Sulis. Their customers include the descendants of Roman soldiers, for after the horrors of Boudicca's rising, it was Roman policy to integrate the soldiery into the population. We would see the dark-skinned offspring of soldiers from Africa, and blond, blue-eyed children of German mercenaries. The jeweller might be making a necklace for a darkly beautiful girl whose grandfather once grew vines by the shores of the Aegean

ABOVE The spire of Walcot church, seen from Hedgemead Park.

Sea, and the potter might have an order for cooking ware from a wealthy farmer of Celtic ancestry, who now is proud to say '*Civis Romanus sum*' – I am a Roman citizen. All are part of the vibrant cultural mix that is Aquae Sulis.

With the retreat of most of the citizens within the walls in the Dark Ages the street loses its sense of community. Later it becomes just a village around the old church of St Swithin, the villagers' lives only occasionally troubled by greater political events. They are more concerned with a good harvest and weather which will not make their struggle to survive any harder than it already is. With the invention of the stagecoach in the seventeenth century, they may watch agog as these lumber down from London, bringing invalids to take the waters. Perhaps, during the years of the Civil War, when the Parliamentarians hold the city, we might see furtive figures heading for a meeting place safely out of town, to plot the King's return. What better venue than a quiet alehouse in Walcot? Is this the reason for the unusual name of the pub near the church – the Hat and Feather – recalling the days of those dashing cavaliers? But as we travel into the eighteenth century, we can see people clearly and can put names to faces. Here we are in 1744, and here too is Mr Sutton, secondhand clothes dealer, on his deathbed. As the neighbours gather round to help the dying man, he raises himself up on one elbow and announces that he wants to

make a confession. To everyone's amazement, he declares that he is not 'he' at all, but a woman who decided to dress as a man at the age of fourteen, following an attempt to 'betray her virtue'. She has been a footman and a drummer in the army, fighting in Scotland during the 1715 uprising. She has even lived with another woman as man and wife for fourteen years. The *Bath Journal*, like any good tabloid newspaper, will trumpet the story in its pages after her death.

In 1764, we see a crowd gathering outside the old church of St Swithin's. Miss Cassandra Leigh is marrying, and marrying beneath her, mutter some of the gossips. Miss Cassandra Leigh does not care. Her husband, even if he is a somewhat impecunious clergyman, is good-looking and intelligent, and the marriage will prove to be a happy one. Thirty-five years later, one of their daughters is in Bath. A pretty woman in her mid-twenties, and dressed in the latest fashion, she trips down Walcot Street, looking for the shop near Walcot church that sells hat decorations cheaply. Fruits such as strawberries, grapes and cherries are much in fashion but they are quite expensive. She finds the shop and comes out bearing a parcel, and she goes home to write to her sister about it. 'Very cheap we found it, but there are only flowers made there, not fruit.' Nevertheless she has bought the flowers, for, as she tells her sister, 'I cannot help thinking that it is more natural to have flowers grow out of the head than

RIGHT In what were once the stables of the Paragon, reclamation and antique businesses have found a home.

fruit. What do you think on that subject?' She smiles to herself. Will her sister take her seriously? She thinks not – the family is noted for its sense of fun. She signs the letter 'Yours affect:ly Jane' and addresses it to her sister, Miss Cassandra Austen, back at the family home in Steventon.

Time moves on and we turn our attention to the other end of the street, to Mr Hunt's yard at the back of the Beehive Inn. The year is 1817 and people are pouring into the yard. Clearly something unusual is going on. Mr Hunt is directing men carrying makeshift scaffolding, while crowds mill about, waiting for some kind of signal. There is an air of excitement, yet apprehension too. Eventually Mr Hunt, or 'Orator' Hunt as he is universally known, waves the assembled throng onward and it starts to make its way slowly down Walcot Street towards the Orange Grove. Does the crowd only number five hundred, as the *Bath Chronicle* will later claim, or is it nearer to Mr Hunt's estimate of twelve to fifteen thousand? They have come to hear him preach a seditious theory – reform of Parliament, with a ballot in which all men can take part. This he plans to do in a city which is one of the rottenest of rotten boroughs, where a mere thirty councillors elect the two Members of Parliament for a city of over thirty thousand souls. The crowd knows that the army and yeomanry are waiting in the Grove. But later we will see all the participants return. The army officers keep their heads and report that, despite the vast numbers, it is a cheerful, well-behaved meeting. Nothing occurs. Two years later Mr Hunt will go up to Manchester to preach the same doctrine. This time eighty thousand people, in holiday mood, will go off to an area outside the city called St Peter's Fields to hear him speak. The soldiers will panic and open fire. Eleven people will die, and hundreds will be injured. The event will go down in history as the Peterloo Massacre.

The years roll by, and whatever reforms there may be bring few benefits to the poor. Mr Charles Dickens, whom we may have glimpsed from our time machine as he trawls the pubs of Bath, gathering material for his novels, has written graphically about their plight. Our next scene, in 1849, is as grim as anything that flows from his pen. Down Walcot Street, heading for the Chatham House, a pub opposite the Bell named after the Whig politician William Pitt, Earl of Chatham, comes a ragged, quarrelsome couple. Clutched in the woman's arms is a tiny bundle, from which, every so often, a plaintive cry may be heard. It is Emma Brockenbrow, just seven days old, whose future will depend on the maternal affection of the drunken figure in whose arms she lies, and on the tenderness of her mother's lover, George Saunders. Neither of these qualities is much in evidence. Grinding poverty makes them a luxury. Alcohol dulls the pain – and the sensibilities. There will be no future for Emma Brockenbrow. Once inside the pub, the two adults start fighting and Emma falls from her mother's arms. They pick her up, but when do they notice she is no longer crying? In the pub or when they get home? Perhaps it is not until they wake from their drunken stupor, to find Emma as stiff and cold as the marble babies which Queen Victoria adds to her art collection in faraway Osborne House. Never a pair to waste good drinking time, the two stumble out again to the pub, and it is only when an acquaintance asks after Emma that the shocked neighbourhood discovers the truth.

By 1903 conditions are improving, and inspectors, engineers and clerks make surveys of houses, sewers and water supplies in an attempt to direct aid to the most needy places. Down Walcot Street comes an official-looking gentleman. He is going in and out of all the pubs, but he is clearly not drinking and he frequently wears a frown. He is Mr E. Newton Fuller, Clerk to the Magistrates, and he is inspecting pubs, paying particular attention to their sanitary arrangements. He comes out of the Walcot Wine Vaults shaking his head and scribbling censoriously in his notebook. If we could look over his shoulder we would find he has written, 'No sanitary accommodation for the public except WC in cellar, approached by trap door in bar'. He looks forward to entering the newly rebuilt Hat and Feather, and being able to enter 'Very good' in his often woeful catalogue. If only more of the landlords would emulate the White Lion at Larkhall and have a separate WC for ladies. He was impressed with that. It also earned a 'Very good', an accolade he awards to very few of Bath's pubs.

We move on to June 2003. It's Walcot Nation Day, and the street, which has been closed to traffic, is filled with people. Despite sporadic rain, spirits have not been dampened, and children, their faces painted to look like tigers, clowns or fairies, are gazing open-mouthed at the colourful array of adults, many of whom have dressed for the occasion or are dancing to the variety of bands playing along the street. The opening parade is graced by Lady Margaret Oswick – better known as Ralph Oswick, artistic director of the Natural Theatre Company. If the ghost of 'Mr' Sutton is watching, this cross-dressing should cause the phantom to smile. Just near the old cornmarket, Walcot's local group, the Zen Hussies, are entertaining the crowds with their unique mixture of Dadaesque cabaret, twenties hits, ska, jazz – and anything else that takes their fancy. On again, and the sound of Northumbrian pipes and the odd cry of 'Ow! that hurt' accompany a group of sword dancers tying themselves into ever more complicated knots. At the top of the street is a band so ecologically friendly that their amplifiers are worked by two people vigorously pedalling a bicycle attached to a generator. All along the street is a bewildering array of food and drink stalls. Indian, Caribbean, Middle Eastern, and the ubiquitous burger – no one should go hungry or thirsty. Most of the businesses have joined in the carnival atmosphere. It is sobering to think that, nearly two thousand years ago, there would have been similar carnivals to celebrate Roman festivals. Certainly, in many ways, Walcot Street has come full circle.

If, on our journey from the old Northgate, we had forked left instead of right at St Michael's church, we would have found ourselves in Broad Street. Some of its buildings date back many centuries, although their earlier history has been hidden behind Georgian frontages. One shop, No. 3, has timber framing at the rear, while another, No. 7, contains within its walls the exterior of the earlier house, complete with windows and a date stone. In the alleyway at the side, a clear join can be seen between the Bath stone ashlar blocks of the eighteenth-century extension and the mixture of lias stone and brick in the old house. There is even an original mullioned window with Cotswold-style dripstones. It is clear that when some of the houses were rebuilt in the early eighteenth century their architects had not quite grasped

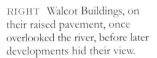

RIGHT Walcot Buildings, on their raised pavement, once overlooked the river, before later developments hid their view.

RIGHT From the roof of the Guildhall there is a fine view of the lopsided Camden Crescent with its five central columns. The slopes of Hedgemead drop away in front of it.

Palladian principles. One house, No. 41, now shorn of its top storey, has its central architectural decoration offset, so that the house looks lopsided. Others combine classical motifs with cottage gables. This arrangement can also be seen in nearby Green Street, which dates from 1716, when it was built on an old bowling green. Broad Street was the home of the city's weaving community, and the vestry of St Michael's had large dye-pots for weavers not wealthy enough to provide their own. Like Walcot Street, Broad Street had a large number of pubs, but of these the Saracen's Head is the sole survivor. It dates back to at least 1728 and may be earlier. The date of 1713 on one of the gables is probably a red herring, as is the information that Charles Dickens stayed here in 1835, as an unknown journalist. To be fair, he must have stayed somewhere when he visited Bath. In later years the landlord sold the chair in which Dickens sat to tourists – on several occasions.

One inn which dated back to the seventeenth century was the Black Swan. In 1744 the landlady, Deborah Chambers, had her lease revoked by the Corporation, who wanted to build a new school on the site. King Edward's School, founded in 1552 and originally in Frog Lane, where New Bond Street now stands, had been moved in 1583 to the nave of the disused church of St Mary by the Northgate, just within the city wall. It was not the ideal location for a school, as it was right next to the market place. In addition to the noise of the traders, there were workshops, one of which was such a nuisance that it was closed by the Corporation at the request of the headmaster. To make matters worse, the tower of the church was the town gaol. Some of these prisoners were tough characters, and their proximity must have been a further worry, especially when they escaped, as often happened. At last the Corporation, prompted by a vigorous headmaster, agreed to build a new school, and the site in Broad Street was selected. Thomas Jelly, a local builder who here proved himself to be a competent architect as well, built the school, which maintained a presence on the site until 1987, when it was sold and the junior school joined the senior school on the outskirts of Bath. This fine Georgian building currently sits dejected and derelict; it is on English Heritage's

RIGHT Broad Street is named after the broad looms of the weavers who once lived here. St Michael's kept dye-pots in the vestry for those weavers who could not afford their own.

'At Risk' register. A campaign is afoot to persuade the Corporation to take it over and make it the Bath Museum. Surprisingly, considering the richness of the city's heritage, it has no museum giving an overall view of its history, although there are many specialist museums.

At the top of the street is the York House Hotel, which was in its day one of the top coaching inns in the country. It was here that Princess Victoria stayed on her visit to Bath. A right turn leads to Bladud's Buildings, a development built in the 1750s on a narrow strip of land called Cockey's Garden. It was the work of Thomas Atwood, the builder and councillor who had been responsible for the skulduggery over the Guildhall. Here one can only admire his boldness, particularly when the buildings are viewed from Walcot Street, where they loom over Ladymead like a cliff. Opposite Bladud's Buildings was once a field called Vineyards or Whynyards, where until the early eighteenth century grapes were grown. Here another row was built, often called Harlequin Row because it was built of brick with stone quoins, giving it the appearance of a jester's motley costume.

The bricks were eventually covered with render marked to look like stone, but the name stuck.

Back on the south side, following on from Bladud's Buildings, comes the Paragon, built from 1769 onwards. (Although maps show the whole street as the Paragon, strictly speaking it is a collection of developments of which the Paragon is but one.) Among the early residents of the Paragon were Mr and Mrs Leigh Perrot, Jane Austen's aunt and uncle, who were in the habit of spending half the year in Bath. It was during their first stay at 1 Paragon, in August 1799, that Mrs Leigh Perrot was accused of shoplifting. For eight months she exchanged the salubrious air of Bath for the stench of Ilminster gaol, refusing, as she could have done at any time during the proceedings, to buy off her accusers. She was triumphantly acquitted, but the slur – and a mystery – remain. In the account of the trial, the evidence from the witnesses appears highly suspect. They cannot remember where they were or what they were doing before or after the incident, but they all know exactly where everyone was and what everyone said for the brief time Mrs Leigh Perrot was

RIGHT The Paragon, where Jane Austen's aunt and uncle used to stay during the summer season. This genteel development overlooked the far livelier Walcot Street.

in the shop. It seems most likely that it was a blackmailing scam by the shopkeeper and some others who, for reasons of their own, wanted to discredit the Leigh Perrots. (Certainly Aunt Leigh Perrot could easily have offended someone. The girls found her very unlovable, unlike her husband, to whom they were much attached.) There are, however, stories that she later stole other things, although the evidence is vague. Was she innocent or was she a kleptomaniac? It is a pointless but addictive discussion which is still pursued today. It is perhaps surprising that the Leigh Perrots kept coming to Bath after this incident. Maybe they felt stopping would be seen as an admission of guilt. Undoubtedly their presence lent weight to the Austens' decision to move to the city in 1801.

33 Paragon was the home of the great actress Sarah Siddons, whose fans wept and fainted while watching her in her most famous roles. It is said that Gainsborough was less impressed while he painted her portrait, enquiring of her, 'Madam, is there no end to your nose?'

Opposite the Paragon stands a building in Strawberry Hill Gothick style. Now the Building of Bath Museum, where visitors can discover the construction methods used in creating Bath's golden terraces, it was built as a chapel in 1765 at the behest of Selina, Countess of Huntingdon. This formidable lady was at one point a follower of John Wesley, but she soon quarrelled with him, and proceeded to set up her own chapels under the title 'The Countess of Huntingdon's Connexion'. Fashionable society at Bath in the late 1760s poured into this chapel, some to worship, but others, like Horace Walpole, to mock. Selina died in 1791, just a few years before Jane Austen came to Bath, but Jane must have heard people talking about her, and it has been suggested that she may have been the model for the autocratic Lady Catherine de Burgh in *Pride and Prejudice*.

Also on the north side of the road, squeezed into a triangular site between the Paragon and Guinea Lane, is the Walcot Schools building. Built in 1840, this accommodated a thousand children – four hundred infants, three hundred girls and three hundred boys. It has now been magnificently restored and converted to flats.

LEFT This path up through Hedgemead Park was once a street between houses. The houses fell down or were demolished after landslips, but the street remained.

RIGHT, CLOCKWISE FROM TOP LEFT The Countess of Huntingdon's Chapel, now the Building of Bath Museum; the end house of the Vineyards and the Walcot Schools building of 1840; Walcot's parish church, St Swithin's, with the verger's house in the foreground.

The last terrace on the south side, before Walcot Church, is Axford's Buildings. Opposite are the precarious slopes of Hedgemead Park, at the top of which, through the trees, can be seen another of Bath's magnificent crescents. Jane Austen readers like to make a pilgrimage up here, for this is where, in *Persuasion*, she placed Sir Walter Elliot and his daughters when they came to live in Bath.

Camden Crescent, which was begun about 1788, was promoted by two Bath physicians, John Symons and Caleb Hillier Parry. We cannot be absolutely certain of the architect, but it seems likely that it was John Eveleigh. There are three good reasons for thinking that this was the case. First, in Eveleigh's ledgers there is an entry for plans and elevations on two houses in the crescent. Second, Dr Parry used Eveleigh to design his house, Summerhill, so he was obviously an architect whom the developer favoured. Third, and perhaps most important, there are strong stylistic resemblances between the crescent and other buildings that we know to be by Eveleigh. These include the platband and crowning entablature which slope gently up towards the centre on each side, disguising the stepping of the windows in groups of three as the ground slopes upwards. Most striking is the use of an odd number of columns beneath the central triangular pediment. This is against all the rules of Palladian architecture and was considered shocking in its day.

The building of Camden Crescent was fraught with difficulties. At an early stage the eastern end had to be abandoned when a landslip carried away some of the houses. The central pediment now sits uneasily about two-thirds of the way along. For some years after the landslip the end house was left as a romantic ruin, until it disappeared one night in a thunderstorm.

Having seen what could happen on these slopes, one would have thought that speculators might have avoided them. However, it seems that their only concern was to get houses up and sell them before they fell down. The hillside below the crescent was soon covered in a mass of housing, some quite decent, some pathetic hovels with a family in every room, like Hooper's Court, where little Emma Brockenbrow's mother lived. In the late 1860s the inevitable happened: the land started to move. Over the next decade there was a series of disastrous landslips. In the end the decision was taken to demolish most of what remained; only

LEFT Camden Crescent and Hedgemead Park, with London Street and part of Walcot Street in the middle foreground.

LEFT Camden: an area of views; of houses clinging to the hillside; and of winding paths.

RIGHT The magnificent but truncated Camden Crescent stands defying gravity on this steep hillside. The five columns beneath the pediment are regarded as an architectural solecism – they are certainly eye-catching.

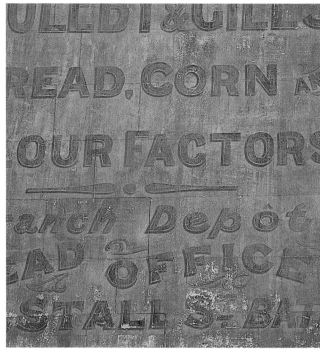

ABOVE LEFT One of the Doric tollhouses on Cleveland Bridge, and beyond it the dispensary of 1845, an early charitable venture into public health care.

ABOVE RIGHT Once every wall was regarded as a potential billboard, as here in Larkhall.

OPPOSITE As banks and builders failed, work stopped, never to be resumed, on Grosvenor Place. Even incomplete, it remains a dazzling example of what can be created out of Bath stone.

Gloster Villas survived. A park was laid out instead and given the original name of the hillside. At least, it is almost the original name. It should be Edgemead – the meadow on the edge – but it became Hedgemead.

Heading eastwards from here the traveller is on London Road. In the days of Aquae Sulis, it was an equally important route for it follows the line of the Fosse Way. Many Roman burial sites have been found along its length. Although it is outside what the tourist considers to be Georgian Bath, there are still many fine eighteenth- and early-nineteenth-century houses along its length, often unnoticed as the motorist copes with the busy traffic. Cleveland Place, where the road comes in from Bathwick, is a confident exercise in Greek Revival by Henry Edmund Goodridge, with fine ironwork. Interestingly, the deeds, which include the architectural plans, were signed at the home of William Beckford, at Lansdown Crescent (see page 195). Grosvenor Place, with its seven central columns, draped in garlands, was designed as the entrance to pleasure gardens where there were to be firework displays and concerts. Sadly, the scheme was abandoned on account of the proximity to the river, from which rose mists and the dreaded damps, not to mention the occasional flood. A close look at the frontage reveals that John Eveleigh's finest façade has never been completed. There are blank stone ovals where there should be pictures of animals, and some of the pillars have plain stone bands which should have been carved into garlands.

Before ending our exploration of this part of Bath, we should make a diversion to Larkhall. This, like Widcombe, Weston and Combe Down, is one of Bath's villages, and retains its sense of community. In its day it too was a spa, and the Greek Revival Pump Room building still stands, although it has been converted to flats. The most interesting building in Larkhall, however, is the Larkhall Inn. This was the original Lark Hall from which the village takes its name. From here one can visit other villages such as Swainswick and Batheaston, or climb up the steep slopes of Little Solsbury, where Prince Bladud is supposed to have held court. There is fine walking in these eastern valleys, but we will turn back and retrace our steps on a journey to Bathwick.

BEYOND THE BRIDGE

THE PULTENEY ESTATE

BEYOND THE BRIDGE

THE PULTENEY ESTATE

PAGES 164–165 Pulteney Bridge, designed by Robert Adam, leads us out of the city and into Bathwick.

OPPOSITE Mist rises from the River Avon as it tumbles over the weir.

To anyone casually glancing at a series of maps showing how Bath grew during the eighteenth century, it may seem surprising that it was so late before building spread other than northwards. A closer examination reveals some contributory geographical features. To the south is not only the river but also the great bluff of Beechen Cliff, both restricting expansion. However, it seems remarkable that there was not further expansion westwards along the road to Bristol, south of the Commons. Hidden away in John Wood's *Description of Bath* is one possible explanation. He says that the Corporation raised the fares of sedan chairs between the Assembly Rooms and the new buildings to the west so that they were double the fare between the Rooms and the extremities of the old city. This, he states, 'restrained the progress of the building to the westward'. Coincidentally, it also played into Wood's hands. The Corporation were apparently so convinced that he would not be able to build to the east, because of the river and its low-lying flood plain, that they did nothing about the fares there, thus making his development of the Parades far more attractive. There is something odd about all this – a feeling that something underhand was going on. There is a suggestion in the *Description of Bath* that Beau Nash was involved in the sedan chair price rise. Certainly the Duke of Kingston was backing Wood's eastward plans, and Nash may also have been a surreptitious supporter.

However, in the latter half of the century, major expansion eastwards began, instigated by the Pulteney family, who owned the fields across the River Avon on the east of the city. They had cast envious eyes at the new developments, and the profits they were bringing to landowners. A plan for building on the eastern fields began to emerge.

The man who proved to be the driving force behind the expansion was William Johnstone Pulteney, a shadowy figure who is better known to Americans than to the English, thanks to his extensive estates and developments there. He was born William Johnstone in 1729, the impoverished second son of a well-connected Scottish family, who took the sensible step of marrying Frances Pulteney, the cousin and heiress of William Pulteney, first Earl of Bath. In 1767, when she inherited vast estates, Johnstone took her name. The first Earl had done nothing with the land he owned in Bathwick, apart from allowing the development of Spring Gardens, a pleasure garden that stood opposite Harrison's Walks.

Johnstone, or William Pulteney as he now was, probably considered himself a canny Scot. At best he was very careful with his money, at worst he could be downright mean. However, he was never afraid to enter into what he saw as a good investment. Unfortunately for Pulteney, members of Bath Corporation were even cannier. His problem was the lack of a bridge across to Bathwick. Without it, his scheme

to develop the estate was doomed to failure. The existing ferries were inadequate, time-consuming and, in times of flood, dangerous. Bridges need approach roads, and Pulteney needed the Corporation's agreement to purchase and demolish the necessary properties. Some of the councillors and other tenants quickly began to demand enormous sums to relinquish their title to the land, while the Corporation looked around to turn Pulteney's scheme to its own advantage. Pulteney had been making plans even before his wife inherited the land, for in 1765 he had acquired the land on which the old prison stood. The Corporation stipulated that if Pulteney wanted to pull the old prison down, he had to build a new one, no further than 300 yards from the east end of his intended bridge.

Pulteney called in his fellow Scot Robert Adam to design the new prison but this plan soon fell through. Once again, as with the Guildhall, Thomas Warr Atwood pulled strings, and the prison was built to his design. The foundation stone was laid in 1772. It looks like a miniature version of a grand mansion, but is very small, only about 20 x 10 metres. One account of the time suggested that so fearful were criminals of being held in the desperately cramped conditions that this kept kept the crime rate down.

Robert Adam, however, did design Pulteney Bridge, though he was not Pulteney's first choice. Pulteney initially gave the job to Timothy Lightoler, the architect who had designed the Octagon Chapel in Milsom Street. The project was subsequently taken over by a Bristol architect, Mr Paty. Work started on the bridge. Then, in 1770, Adam was invited to put forward a design. This was based on Palladio's plan for the Rialto Bridge in Venice, which had been rejected in favour of Antonio da Ponte's design. It had shops on it, and Pulteney realized this would bring in added revenue, which he urgently needed. This time Pulteney did not consult the councillors, probably fearing that if he did they would veto the plan. They were indeed dismayed when they saw it, but by then construction of the new bridge was well under way. They complained that 'the circulation of air will be prevented . . . if a concourse of people constantly pass over it, which must be the case before the shops can be of any value, the dimensions of the bridge will then be too narrow to make the passage convenient.' Their comments were to prove prophetic, but the intervention came too late. Pulteney had enough clout to push ahead regardless, and enough income to finance the bridge until the trustees of the estate arranged for more Acts of Parliament to permit further borrowing.

Although we cherish the bridge today, when it was built it was regarded as outdated. Bridges with shops on were being demolished, not built. It was approached by huge

ABOVE The elegant parade of Great Pulteney Street, epitomizing the ideal of Regency Bath.

causeways on either side to raise it above flood levels. Some idea of their height can be gained by walking through the archway leading from Grove Street to Spring Gardens Road, at the east end of the bridge. Until the houses were built, the causeways were unfenced, making them dangerous, especially at night. The bridge was expensive to build, finally costing nearly £11,000, over £1,000,000 in today's terms. Worse, once the bridge was complete in 1774, Pulteney could not find tenants for the shops. The American War of Independence had brought a slump, and it was not until the 1780s that the city's fortunes revived.

When this revival occurred, Adam submitted plans for the rest of the estate but Pulteney, probably again under pressure from the Corporation, turned to the City Architect, Thomas Baldwin, instead. Baldwin intended Great Pulteney Street to be a central spine, with gardens in an irregular hexagon at its centre. The section of the street east of the gardens was to be called Upper Great Pulteney Street. The first problem was to find a way to expand from the narrowness of the bridge to the width of Great Pulteney Street. The solution is less than ideal. The bridge leads into Argyle Street, which is wider than the bridge, and this leads into Laura Place, named after Pulteney's daughter, Henrietta Laura Pulteney. Laura Place allows the final expansion into Great Pulteney Street itself, 1000 feet long and 100 feet wide.

The estate was to be a celebration of the Pulteney family and its connections. In addition to Laura Place, there is Henrietta Street, William Street and Johnstone Street. There was also to be Frances Square, in honour of Henrietta's mother, who had died in 1782. The estate had devolved to her daughter, with William Johnstone Pulteney having a life interest, and it was Henrietta who issued the first building leases in 1788. Work at first proceeded quickly, but then the economic crisis triggered by war with France brought the development to a halt. Upper Great Pulteney Street and Frances Square were never built. Great Annandale Street was supposed to run parallel with Great Pulteney Street, and there was to be a crescent facing the city from the Bathwick side. None of it was ever constructed. Sunderland Street can claim to be Bath's shortest street, leading only to Henrietta Park, where Frances Square was meant to be. Johnstone Street leads to the recreation ground, the site of the intended crescent. However, the gardens proposed as the centre of the development were laid out, opening in 1795 as Sydney Gardens Vauxhall. Only two of the six intended streets around the hexagon were completed, however: Sydney Place and New Sydney Place.

At the time when work first started on Bathwick New Town, there were already two sets of pleasure gardens on the east side of the river: Spring Gardens, dating from 1742, and

ABOVE LEFT The doorway of a house in one of the intended linking streets – now going nowhere.

ABOVE RIGHT The coat of arms of Henrietta Laura Pulteney, Countess of Bath.

Bathwick Villa, dating from 1779. Spring Gardens lay close to the river, looking across to the Abbey. Visitors reached it either from the ferry upstream, or by a 'commodious pleasure boat' supplied by the proprietors. In 1766, the Reverend John Penrose described the gardens as 'a most delightful spot laid out in gravel and grass walks, some straight, others serpentine, with a fine canal in one place and a fine pond in another'. The canal was a long straight pond, and the whole garden seems to have been in the formal Dutch style. The garden at Westbury on Severn, owned by the National Trust, is almost the only survivor of this type of garden. Spring Gardens contained a large building which was popular for public breakfasts. Among the items on the menu were Spring Gardens Rolls, for which Miss Sally Lunn acquired the franchise around 1780 (a hundred years later than the date given in the shop which bears her name). It was after this that they became known as Sally Lunns. Regular features of the gardens were firework displays, concerts and novelty acts such as that of Signor Rossignol, who imitated birdsong. The proprietors benefited for a time from the new bridge, but once building work began in earnest the dust made it less attractive and the estate began to encroach on its northern limits.

Bathwick Villa, lying just to the east of the old village of Bath Wick, laid on similar events – fireworks, concerts, even riding displays – but its history was a little unusual. James Ferry, a silk mercer who had had a shop in the Parades, was also an alderman. It was he who built the house, which was, like the Countess of Huntingdon's Chapel, in Strawberry Hill Gothick. Amy Frost, administrator of Beckford's Tower, has made a strong case for the two buildings having had the same – unknown – architect.

It was the interior of Bathwick Villa that was particularly strange, and we know about it thanks to a visit by Fanny Burney. She and her friends were kept out in the garden while the house was prepared, after which they were taken through 'four or five little vulgarly showy closets, not rooms' before being led into 'a very gaudy little apartment, where the master of the house sat reclining on his arm'. It was meant to look as though he had been caught quietly contemplating, although it was all part of what proved to be a rather bizarre performance. First of all there was a sort of peepshow involving ships, boats and water. Then a trap door opened and 'up jumped a covered table, ornamented with various devices'. After they had admired this, 'down dropped an eagle from the ceiling, whose talons were put into a certain hook at the top of the covering of the table, and when the admiration was over, up again flew the eagle, conveying in his talons the cover, and leaving under it a repast of cakes, sweetmeats, oranges and jellies.' The final effect was the disappearing housemaid, who, having sat in an armchair, sank underground to be replaced with 'a barber's block with a vast quantity of black wool on it and a high headdress.' Fanny Burney's party laughed all the way home.

Sadly for Mr Ferry, he had over-reached himself financially. The villa had to be mortgaged. Then he had to resign his post as City Chamberlain because he failed to balance the accounts – although he had sufficient friends on the Corporation to be awarded a pension of £100 a year (something like £10,000 today). Bathwick Villa and its grounds were auctioned and run for a time by a wine merchant from Milsom Street. The villa was also affected by the building works, for although it was some distance from the work in progress, the journey became unpleasantly dusty. By the time it was demolished in 1897 it had been turned into tenements, and the grounds had become a shanty town of labourers' houses.

Sydney Gardens Vauxhall was a far more sophisticated affair. For a start, it had a properly designed entrance, and there were plans for equally grand side entrances. Hopes of improving Bath's flagging fortunes had been pinned on the

summer season becoming as important as the winter season, but this never happened. Thomas Baldwin designed a light, airy house, almost like an orangery, as an entrance to the gardens, but by this time he was already sinking into severe financial difficulties. It was the surveyor and mapmaker Charles Harcourt Masters who took over Baldwin's plans. He ignored his predecessor's inspired design – perhaps he felt it was too unconventional – and produced something quite different. It was certainly not new, however. He simply copied Baldwin's design for the Guildhall, now twenty years old, and pulled forward the central section to act as a *porte-cochère*. Inside were reception rooms, including a coffee room, cardroom and reading room, where the latest newspapers were available. It was soon apparent that using the building simply as an entrance would not generate sufficient income to keep it viable, and it became a hotel 'for families of distinction'. The side entrances were also abandoned in the interests of economy.

The gardens were also a series of 'rooms' – here a bowling green, there a miller's cottage with water-wheel, a

RIGHT The Kennet and Avon Canal as it passes through Sydney Gardens is crossed by a bridge 'in the manor of the Chinese'. Beyond it is Cleveland House, once the head office of the Kennet and Avon Canal Company.

labyrinth (laid out by 'an intelligent native of Scotland') and a rill which flowed down through various of these stage-managed settings. One formal aspect was a straight central path, but the rest was designed to surprise and delight. Events were arranged for both day and night. At one '*grand fête champêtre*' in 1804 not less than twelve hundred persons sat down to an elegant breakfast. Even greater crowds attended the gala nights when, after the concert, over five thousand 'variegated lamps' would be lit in the grounds and the evening would conclude with the inevitable firework display. There was a boost to the gardens' finances in 1800, when the Kennet and Avon Canal Company sought permission to cut through them. Grudgingly, the proprietors gave their permission. The Canal Company had to pay the large sum of 2,000 guineas (nearly £250,000 in modern terms) and build bridges, designed 'in the manner of the Chinese', across the canal. It must have been a constant irritation to the Company, having complied with these onerous demands, to find the canal advertised as one of the garden's attractions.

A less appealing intrusion was that of the Great Western Railway, opened in 1841. The section through the gardens was designed by Brunel to look like a stage set. He even constructed one of the bridges across the railway in iron, in imitation of the canal bridges. But proud though Brunel was of his trains, the public found them noisy and dirty. Moreover, the railway destroyed one of the favourite features of the garden, the labyrinth.

With the coming of the railway, the gardens' fortunes faded. The hotel was sold off by 1843, and a wall was built, cutting it off from the gardens. It was converted to a hydropathic establishment and later a school. Eventually even the school left and for a while it stood derelict, until, in 1913, it was bought by the trustees of the Holburne of Menstrie Collection. The architect Reginald Blomfield removed all that was left of the old Sydney Hotel, leaving only the façade, and created a purpose-built gallery which opened in 1916. The Holburne Museum now houses a wonderful collection of paintings, porcelain, furniture and other *objets d'art*, mainly, though not exclusively, from the

RIGHT Sabrina, spirit of the Severn, guards the portal of the western canal tunnel, where the canal leaves the gardens.

LEFT, ABOVE The reconstruction of the Temple of Minerva, erected in Sydney Gardens to commemorate the pageant of 1909.

LEFT, BELOW The *porte-cochère* of Sydney House.

RIGHT Sydney House, now the Holburne Museum.

ABOVE, LEFT TO RIGHT
Jane Austen lived at 4 Sydney
Place; New Sydney Place climbs
the hillside; in Regency times
these covered balconies became
fashionable.

Georgian period. It has frequent special exhibitions, and has a lively series of children's events, lectures and concerts. The building has once again become an important part of Bath life. The gardens, too, after many years of sinking into a quiet retirement, may spring to life, as the museum and the Parks Department are working together on a project to restore some of the original features of the pleasure grounds and reintegrate the museum building into the garden landscape.

From the door of the Holburne Museum there is a wonderful vista straight up Great Pulteney Street. Today the houses along the street tend to be hotels, retirement homes or flats; when they were first built many were lodging-houses of the highest quality. Those in Laura Place were held in particularly high regard. This is where, in *Persuasion*, Jane Austen places the Viscountess, Lady Dalrymple, before whom the snobbish Sir Walter Elliot and his elder daughter Elizabeth grovel. The Austens themselves lived for a time at 4 Sydney Place, facing Sydney Gardens. Jane, who was very unhappy at the decision to move to Bath, made the best of it, saying that they would not starve, for they could always go to the public breakfasts in the gardens. In *Bath Tangle*, Georgette Heyer, Jane Austen's twentieth-century disciple, lodges her wealthiest heroines in Laura Place, while in *Black Sheep*, the book in which she most closely imitated the

Austen style, she locates her heroine, Miss Abigail Wendover, in Sydney Place.

Sydney Place, to the west of the gardens, is plainer than Great Pulteney Street, but still has a strong design, and was part of Baldwin's original plan. Eventually, however, Baldwin's financial juggling failed him and he was declared bankrupt. New Sydney Place, which runs along the south-east side of the gardens, is somewhat later, and was designed by John Pinch, who had replaced Baldwin as surveyor to the Bathwick estate.

Many consider Pinch at his best to be Bath's most accomplished architect. While he never built great showpieces like the Circus or Queen Square, his treatment of Bath's difficult terrain was far more successful than that of any other architect, with the possible exception of John Eveleigh. He led the way in the change from terraces to villas. Furthermore, unlike many other architects and developers, he expected a high standard of workmanship. New Sydney Place is not quite his finest achievement, but an account of 1808, quoted by Walter Ison in *The Georgian Buildings of Bath 1700–1830*, gives an indication that, even in this city with so many golden terraces, it was regarded as something out of the ordinary. It was described as 'a specimen of the architectural perfection that may be formed of Bath stone. It was all brought from one quarry, and the houses raised

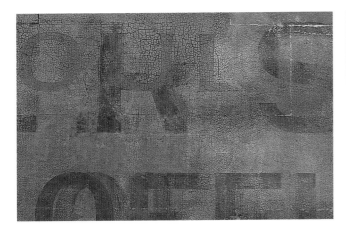

ABOVE More examples of the sign-writer's skills.

gradually together, tier after tier, thereby forming one compact building in which not the least flaw or settlement, or different shades of colour can be seen.' Here for the first time Pinch used a trick to deal with the progression of the houses climbing the hillside that became his trademark. Instead of simply stepping them as the Woods had done, or using a sloping platband as Eveleigh did at Camden Crescent and Somerset Place, he swept all the cornices and string courses up in a quadrant where they met the next house. At Cavendish Place he was to do this with great boldness, but New Sydney Place was the first experiment, and it must have seemed astonishing. The houses are built to a very high quality. The walls are lined with brick, and some have curved doors to the ground floor rooms. These are solid, and must have been steamed in a barrel to be coaxed into this shape. No wonder that when Queen Charlotte and her retinue came to Bath in 1817, this is where they stayed.

The account of New Sydney Place also mentions settlement. One of the problems of the Bathwick estate was flooding. Although the houses were raised up quite high, some having sub-basements and even sub-sub-basements, the ground had a tendency to become boggy whenever the river rose. A look along the roofline reveals that there has indeed been settlement, as the parapets can be seen to follow a wavering route.

Like other developments we have looked at, Bathwick had a proprietary chapel. It stood at the back of Henrietta Street and was known as Laura Chapel. Its design was unusual in being a perfect ellipse. It seated a thousand, and was almost certainly the chapel attended by the Austens when they lived in Sydney Place. Sadly, by 1900 it was derelict and on the point of collapse. There were considerable arguments about its future, some people saying it was unsafe, others arguing that as it was an ellipse it could not fall down because the stones could not fall inwards and would not fall outwards. Perhaps fortunately, this bizarre theory was never put to the test. The building was demolished; only its entrances remain.

Slowly building work edged towards the old village of Bath Wick, clustered around its little parish church. The east side of Bathwick Street was completed in the early 1790s but after just two or three houses had been finished in Daniel Street in 1789, the side streets were abandoned, and it was not until 1810 that the rest of the street was completed, to a less ambitious but still elegant design of Pinch's. Some of the old houses were 'Georgianized' and absorbed into the plan, but the biggest problem was the church. It simply was not big enough. John Pinch was commissioned by William Henry Vane, third Earl of Darlington, who inherited the Bathwick estate in 1808, to design a church to accommodate fourteen hundred people. What he produced was St Mary's Bathwick, Bath's first true Gothic Revival building. The tower recalls some of the finest Somerset Perpendicular church towers and the church bears more than a passing resemblance to Bath Abbey. In the interior, comfort was as important as appearance. It was advertised as being heated by flues, 'so that persons of the most delicate health may visit the church in perfect safety'. The church bears the date of 1820, which is when it was consecrated.

Near by is one of Bath's few Art Deco buildings – the fire station. This dates from the mid 1930s. The city's coat of arms above the garage door is flanked by helmets and hosepipes rampant. The tower is also part of the original design, although its leaded windows have been sacrificed for practicality.

This part of Bath is rich in unusual architecture. In front of a modern, and decidedly undistinguished, block of flats, is a gateway that appears to date from the seventeenth century. This was erected by a member of the Pinch family, although even descendants of the Pinches seemed to be a little confused as to who was responsible – John Pinch the Elder, his son, also John, or his grandson William. William seems the most likely since he lived at Rochford Place, next to the gateway. The puzzling question is where it came from.

The theory is that it was reclaimed from a site on which the family was working, and erected here.

The nearby tollhouses on Cleveland Bridge, dating from 1827, are splendid examples of Greek Revival. This is one of Bath's two iron road bridges. (The other is North Parade Bridge, its iron construction now sadly hidden by stone and concrete.) William Henry Vane, who had been created Marquis of Cleveland that very year (and was to be elevated to become the first Duke of Cleveland in 1833), decided that the obvious way to bring more people to Bathwick was to build another bridge across the river. This had been part of William Pulteney's original plan. Indeed, he had hoped to make Great Pulteney Street the principal road into Bath, but once again he had been foiled by the Corporation. John Pinch put forward plans for a bridge in 1810 and 1822, as did John Rennie, the Kennet and Avon Canal Company's engineer, and Thomas Telford, who had been William Pulteney's protégé. It was Henry Edmund Goodridge who finally provided the successful design. As his father, James Goodridge, was agent for Vane, was this nepotism? Or was William Beckford, Goodridge's patron, pulling strings with his aristocratic friends to get Goodridge the job? Whatever the reason, this is one of Bath's best bridges, and continues

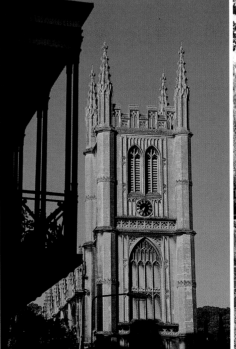

to serve the city well today, carrying far more and far heavier traffic than any of its originators could have dreamt of.

Pinch and Goodridge also meet on Bathwick Hill. At first Pinch continued to build terraces, such as Raby Place, but with an eye to modern trends he turned to villas. A stroll up Bathwick Hill or Lansdown Hill provides an object lesson in how architectural taste developed throughout the eighteenth and nineteenth centuries. As we walk up Bathwick Hill, so Pinch gives way to Goodridge. Woodland Place, with its strict Greek Revival proportions, influenced by Sir John Soane, is an easily missed gem. Towards the top of the hill we come to the Italianate villas of the 1840s. This style also developed as the century moved on. Cleveland Walk, which links Bathwick Hill with North Road, has late-Victorian houses that ooze confidence and wealth, and say much about the attitudes of the time. These vast houses, even more than their Georgian predecessors, needed armies of servants to run them.

Having reached North Road, we discover first of all King Edward's School. The senior school decamped to green fields in the 1960s, and the junior school, a hidden jewel of practical modern architecture, joined it in the 1980s. A further climb brings us to another educational establishment, Bath University, which began life as the Bristol College of Science and Technology. Bristol Council was alarmed by the size of the proposed expansion of the college, and procrastinated over granting planning permission. Bath Corporation was only too happy to offer a site, particularly as this type of college was being offered university status by the government. By 1966, Bath had achieved an ambition it had cherished for over a hundred years. It was a university city.

From the university one can pick up the Skyline Walk, a series of footpaths across land administered largely by the National Trust. It affords some spectacular vistas of the north of the city, and it is northwards that we head for the final chapter.

ARCADIAN LANDSCAPES

THE PLEASURES OF THE PICTURESQUE

ARCADIAN LANDSCAPES
THE PLEASURES OF THE PICTURESQUE

ABOVE A vine grows over one of the overthrows, or lamp-irons, at Lansdown Crescent.

PAGES 180–181 Lansdown Crescent appears above its Arcadian setting of sheep safely grazing. The development began as a single house (at extreme right). It was three years before the developers began to expand it into a crescent.

OPPOSITE The western end of the crescent, showing Beckford's bridge linking No. 20 with No. 1 Lansdown Place West.

We have already seen that as Bath grew, it changed in other ways. The increased infrastructure necessary to support the burgeoning tourist trade brought new problems, while wars and economic recessions caused fluctuations in the city's popularity and prosperity. Alongside extreme wealth came extreme poverty. But the driving force for change in a city devoted to pleasure was fashion. If one thing is constant it is that fashion always changes: absorbing the new, looking back and adapting the old, sometimes gradually developing, sometimes violently reacting to what has gone before. So it was in eighteenth- and nineteenth-century Bath. Not only did society demand new entertainments, it also became bored with styles of design in architecture and decoration. During the second half of the eighteenth century archaeological discoveries at Pompeii and Split revealed that Roman domestic architecture was far lighter than the heavy formality adopted by Palladio, and was full of colour. Young men returned from the Grand Tour with their minds reeling from the dramatic scenery and their baggage full of works of art. Ideas about the picturesque – already seen to be influential during the building of the Royal Crescent – took a firm hold on the imaginations of those who wished to be trendsetters. Where earlier architects had had to persuade fashionable society to move out to a semi-rural location, now there was a positive demand for *rus in urbe* – the countryside in the town.

By 1785 two Bath developers, a banker called John Lowder and a coachmaker called Charles Spackman, had taken a tentative step to test the market by building a single house on the western-facing slopes of Lansdown. It was reasonable to assume that this might become a fashionable area. The Hon. Charles Hamilton had already built Rock House on one side of the Lansdown Road. Opposite him was an older house, referred to on the maps as Mr Lloyd's house (it is now the central part of the Lansdown Grove Hotel). It too was surrounded by extensive grounds.

Whether Spackman and Lowder always intended to build a crescent is uncertain. The indications are that they did not. The interior layout of that first house, which later became 1 Lansdown Crescent, is substantially different from that of the other houses and matching it successfully with the rest of the crescent presented many problems. If the thought had crossed their minds, the difficulties faced by Eveleigh at Camden must have made them pause. However, although the gradient here was far greater than that at the Royal Crescent, it was certainly not as precipitous as at Hedgemead. They decided to press ahead with a new crescent, began purchasing the necessary land, and in 1787 placed a notice in the *Bath Chronicle* advertising their intention. This stated that a plan would be laid before the principal builders for their approbation. 'In the meantime,'

LEFT Lansdown Place East, early on a winter morning. The field in front of the crescent was called Hilly Lydes.

PAGES 186–187 The view from High Common showing Cavendish Crescent with Lansdown Crescent in the distance. In the foreground is a modern pseudo-Georgian block of retirement homes on the controversial Cavendish Lodge site. It sits unhappily among the crescents of Georgian Bath.

ABOVE Somerset Place, Eveleigh's last fling in Bath. It is notable for its segmental broken pediment, decorated with garlands.

the advertisement continued, 'it is requested that they will take a survey of the ground and house already built on the spot . . . a person will attend at the house, Lansdown Place, to shew the ground. There are very fine springs of water in the ground and plenty of fine stone and sand.'

The question left unanswered by this advertisement is, which architect drew the plan? John Palmer has often been suggested, but so far no evidence connects him with the site. One strong claimant must be John Lowder himself. Family history suggests that he was a gentleman architect – he was reputed to have designed the odd little roundhouse in Devon called À la Ronde, dating from 1795. Certainly his son, also called John, was a professional architect and carried out work for Bath Corporation. Whoever the architect of Lansdown Crescent was, he used as the basis for his design the 'Line of Beauty', a serpentine shape described by Hogarth, in his *Analysis of Beauty* of 1753, as a line of grace or elegance 'which leads the eye and mind a wanton kind of chase'. It was perfect for the undulating hillside, and nothing quite like it had ever been seen before. The Royal Crescent looks stiff and formal by comparison. The steep hillside in front of the crescent meant that it commanded, as the original advertisement said, 'a most beautiful and extensive prospect of near twenty miles to the south and south west'. Work began in 1788 and by 1795 the whole crescent and the two adjoining wings were complete.

In 1794 a chapel, dedicated to All Saints, was also built for the use of residents. This too is generally attributed to Palmer but if so it is unlike anything else he did. This time, it is possible that the younger Lowder was responsible – he certainly lived in the house on its eastern side, and he was the architect of the now-vanished Holy Trinity Church, James Street, which bore strong stylistic similarities to All Saints. As with many proprietary chapels, it was a business enterprise: the initial financing was by the issue of twenty shares, the shareholders being referred to as proprietors.

One of them was Robert St John Lucas, manager of Bath's smartest hotel, the York House, at the bottom of Lansdown Hill. His two shares entitled him to two whole pews, and it is probable that these were for the use of his hotel guests. The income for running the chapel was provided by pew rents, and places were carefully allocated. There were, however, complaints that servants sometimes occupied pews that were not intended for them. Money was a constant worry for the proprietors, who were keen to see a return on the £5,500 they had spent on the chapel.

Although Lansdown Crescent was classical in its decoration, the chapel was built in a kind of Strawberry Hill Gothick, with a mass of little pinnacles and a rather stumpy tower. Considered in isolation, the design looks rather strange, but it was all part of the plan to help the viewer

appreciate the scenery. The top of the tower was at the eye level of anyone standing in the crescent, drawing the attention of the admiring spectator away from the city of Bath to the green hills of Somerset in the distance. This was truly *rus in urbe*. Today, although the church has gone, the crescent still stands, while sheep graze in the field below. It is a perfect Georgian prospect, demonstrating the ideal of elegance and order set among and integrating with the natural landscape. It also shows how important space was to Georgian designers. Spackman and Lowder went to great trouble to secure the land in front of the crescent to complement and enhance its appearance.

Shortly after work started on Lansdown Crescent, John Eveleigh put forward plans for a new development on a site to the west. Eveleigh may perhaps have noticed the possibilities of the location as he went to visit Philip Thicknesse, who was now living at a nearby cottage called the Hermitage. This was not grandiose enough for him and he employed Eveleigh to build an extension. The path to the Hermitage would have taken the architect directly past the field where he now proposed a new building. His idea initially seems to have been quite simple: a mansion which would actually be a pair of houses. As ever with Eveleigh, the design was bold and innovative. Instead of the more usual triangular pediment, he crowned it with a huge segmental arch, running

across the frontage of the two houses. The arch is broken in the middle, with a vase at the centre point where the ends of two reversed arches meet. The space beneath is filled with festooned drapery, ribbons and paterae. This theme is used more delicately as a central feature on lower floors, and then, in each of the keystones of the two doorways, there is a grotesque face in icicle carving. Locals insist that these were used by the stonemasons to commemorate a severe winter. It is true that this type of decoration, which Eveleigh also used at Grosvenor Place, was decidedly *passé* by the 1790s, when there was indeed a series of very hard winters. Who knows? It is a charming story which ought to be true.

Had Eveleigh left it at that, all might have been well, but he too went on to add flanking wings, developing the building into a crescent, which was given the name of Somerset Place. This time the problems he and his builders faced were not with the terrain but with finance. Food prices rocketed as the severe weather caused shortages, and in the aftermath of the French Revolution there was a general sense of unease. Then came the Napoleonic Wars. This all led to financial instability and, for the first time in the century, inflation. Bankruptcies followed. Several banks collapsed, and builders and developers were caught up in the débâcle. A melancholy advertisement in the local paper for 1793 advertised an auction of the property of William Wheeler, a bankrupt.

Three lots were of complete or near-complete houses in Lansdown Crescent, but there were also three 'skeletons' of houses in the process of construction, including 14 Somerset Place. Wheeler was not alone. In 1794 Eveleigh had to present his ledgers to his creditors. It would be over twenty years before Somerset Place was completed, and even then the western end was shorter than the other. Yet it is a fascinating structure. As at Camden, the stepping of the houses is disguised by a sloping platband across the façade. As the doorways move away from the centre, the keystones become less elaborate, till at the very ends they are completely plain. Somerset Place combines with Lansdown Crescent to make this one of the most visually exciting parts of Bath. From the air, the two crescents together can be seen as a great double Hogarthian curve, snaking across the hillside.

With the building of Somerset Place, the day of the continuous terrace had almost come to an end. Eveleigh's initial plan for a semi-detached villa was the shape of things to come. The nineteenth-century architectural encyclopaedist J.C. Loudon seized on this style of building and is often credited with having invented it, but Bath's John Pinch was very successful with it a good thirty years before Loudon. He is almost certainly the architect of 1 and 2 Winifred's Dale, a semi-detached pair of houses which overlook High Common. However, he did not give up on the terrace,

building the row of thirteen houses called Cavendish Place below Winifred's Dale. Once again Pinch used the technique of curving the cornices as he had in New Sydney Place, but here the design is bolder and more successful. The terrace ripples down the hillside, and on summer evenings, when the stonework turns golden in the light of the setting sun, it is an unforgettable sight.

Cavendish Crescent, higher up the slope, is more severe. A mere quadrant instead of a full crescent, for the first time it brings the attic storey into the design instead of hiding it behind a balustrade. It still has some classical features around the windows of the *piano nobile*, and there is rustication around the doorways, but its bold, strong lines have a very modern feel.

One of Pinch's finest works is to be found further up Lansdown. This is Sion Hill Place. The building leases for it were granted in 1811, and it was developed by a consortium which included the doctor Caleb Hillier Parry, who lived near by in a house called Summerhill, and a former coachbuilder called John Hensley, who had kept his head – and his wealth – while all around were losing theirs. Here, as at Cavendish Crescent, it is the form and proportion of the building which make it so arresting. Decoration is kept to a minimum, although the ironwork on the balconies is a crucial part of the design. Once again the space in front is an important

part of the overall plan, and restrictions were placed on what could be done with the lawn.

Sion Hill Place has an unexpected secret. A much earlier façade has been added to the western end. This spoils the symmetry of the terrace, but if Ernest Cook, son of Thomas Cook the travel agent, had not saved it, a design of the very early eighteenth century might have been lost for ever. It was originally on the front of Benjamin Haskin Stiles's house at Bowden Hill. He fell into debt, and his new house, started in 1721, was never finished. The façade then started on its travels. Some time in the 1750s it was purchased by a clothier called Thomas Figgins for his new house in Chippenham High Street. It stayed there until 1933, when it was decided to demolish the building to erect a new Woolworth's store. The builders employed to do this, Messrs Blackford and Son of Calne, were so horrified at what they were required to do that they placed advertisements in local papers, offering to mark the stones and provide drawings so that it could be re-erected. They would even store the stone if necessary. It is greatly to their credit that they took this remarkable step. Ernest Cook bought the façade, which was shipped to Axford's Yard in Bath and put on view before being reconstructed on the end of Sion Hill Place, where it is now safe. Local author Isabel Ide, who has carried out extensive research into the provenance of the façade, suggests that the architect was probably the Italian Giacomo Leone, who was employed by Haskin Stiles at his house at Moor Park in Hertfordshire.

Sion Hill Place was one of the last Georgian developments on the northern side of Bath. There were two principal reasons for this. First, Bath itself was being abandoned by fashionable society. In 1811, the Prince of Wales became Prince Regent. Now the power was in his hands, the fashionable followed him to his favourite resort of Brighton. Doctors recommended sea-bathing, and even drinking sea water in preference to mineral water. The Royal Pavilion, rebuilt to a design by John Nash, made Bath's classical architecture look staid and outmoded. Georgette Heyer's Regency novels set in Bath accurately portray its genteel slide into boring respectability. Maiden ladies seek retirement there, characters of the high ton refer to it as dull, young ladies are introduced into polite society there before being let

LEFT The central house of Pinch's supremely elegant Sion Hill Place, a model of Regency simplicity.

RIGHT The early-eighteenth-century façade from Chippenham which has been added to the western end of Sion Hill Place.

loose on the delights and dangers of London and Brighton, and the Assembly Rooms are mocked for their failure to include the latest daring dance, the waltz.

From 1824 onwards, there was another reason for Bath's failure to expand northwards beyond Sion Hill Place. For about a mile from Lansdown Crescent to the crest of the hill, most of the land on the west side of the turnpike road, and in places on both sides of the road, was under the control of one man: William Beckford. His arrival in Bath was the culmination of a strange and sometimes scandalous odyssey.

William Beckford was born in 1760, the son of the man who was reputedly England's richest commoner, 'Alderman' William Beckford. Alderman Beckford's family had owned sugar estates in Jamaica since the seventeenth century, and he had been born and brought up there. Unperturbed by mockery of his pronounced Jamaican accent, he made fiery speeches in the House of Commons in support of Pitt. He was famous for promoting constitutional reform, despite representing a rotten borough. He harangued George III to his face about the rights of his people and his poor choice of ministers. He had seven illegitimate children, but in 1756, at

the age of forty-seven, he married, somewhat unexpectedly, Maria Marsh, the widow of a fellow Jamaican merchant. She was fifteen years younger than her new husband, and had an eight-year-old daughter. Four years after the marriage, William the younger was born. The boy was nine when the Alderman died of rheumatic fever.

No two men could have been more different than the Alderman and his son. The former was bluff, enthusiastically heterosexual, and a shrewd businessman. William, brought up at Fonthill in Wiltshire by his pious mother, had an artistic temperament, and was far more attracted to men than women. He was also not in the least interested in the sugar trade. However, for all his dabbling in poetry, art and music, the younger William was in his way as fearless as his father.

At Beckford's twenty-first birthday party, held at Fonthill, and attended by, among others, his fiancée, Lady Margaret Gordon, his life looked full of promise. But problems were looming. He was already in the throes of a love affair with his thirteen-year-old cousin William Courtenay, who lived at Powderham Castle in Devon. The money from the sugar estates was being whittled away in

RIGHT Beckford's Tower. The idea of combining Grecian and Italian motifs may well have been inspired by what Beckford had seen in Venice. In the foreground are the Gates of Death.

RIGHT The Embattled Gateway, which led from Beckford's kitchen garden at Lansdown Crescent to the open down.

lawsuits and embezzled by his fraudulent agents, the Wildman brothers. One thing still working in Beckford's favour was his happy marriage to the woman he undoubtedly loved. He and Lady Margaret were married in May 1783. By May the following year she had miscarried one child and given birth to a stillborn boy, but by July 1784 she was pregnant again. In October they made an ill-fated visit to Powderham that was to go far towards wrecking their lives. It was after they had returned to Fonthill that someone – almost certainly Courtenay's uncle Lord Loughborough, who, for political reasons, detested Beckford – leaked rumours to the press about an incident in Courtenay's bedroom, involving Beckford. If Beckford had been charged and found guilty of homosexuality, he would have risked the death penalty. Lady Margaret, wrongly as it turned out, was said to be suing for divorce. In fact Lady Margaret fiercely defended her husband, and refused to abandon him. After the birth of their first daughter, Maria, the Beckfords went into exile. A year later, Lady Margaret died, giving birth to their second daughter, Susan. Beckford remained abroad for many years (during this time he made a famous garden at Sintra in Portugal). At last he returned home to Fonthill and began the work on the Gothic abbey for which he is best known. By 1822, however, his financial situation was precarious and it was clear that he could no longer sustain his extravagant life-style. Like his great-uncle Charles Hamilton, he decided to retire to Bath.

At first he thought about moving to Prior Park, which was for sale, but he considered the price too high. He then looked across town, and bought 20 Lansdown Crescent. He would have known the area from visiting Charles Hamilton at Rock House. A dedicated garden designer, who had been almost bankrupted by his landscape garden at Painshill in Surrey, Hamilton had purchased a plot of land called Nic Hooper's Tyning and turned it into a kitchen garden with terraces and vaults. After Lansdown Crescent was built in front of it, Spackman and Lowder bought the garden with a view to developing it as Lansdown Square.

This was never built and John Lowder junior, who was architect for Bath's National Schools, allowed the school to use it as a kitchen garden, and possibly to train children in gardening skills. It seems that flax was grown there, for there was equipment on the site to prepare it ready for weaving, and looms, where the children were taught to weave. By 1823 John's brother Charles Lowder had turned it into a pleasure

garden which he put on the market in 1825. It was then that Beckford bought the land, together with the adjacent plot.

Beckford's house and garden, even with the extra land, soon proved too small for him. He bought up other property and took leases on other plots, mainly from the Gunning family who owned much of Lansdown. His first acquisition was 1 West Wing (as Lansdown Place West was then known), which he bought from Ann Lowder, John Lowder senior's widow. He commissioned the young architect Henry Edmund Goodridge to build a bridge between 20 Lansdown Crescent and 1 West Wing (although it was never possible to pass between the houses through the archway). However, by some time in late 1830 or early 1831 Beckford had quitted Lansdown Place West.

For about five years 20 Lansdown Crescent remained his sole residence, but in 1836 Beckford appears in the ratebooks as the occupier of No. 19 as well. Eventually, in the last year of his life, he also occupied No. 18. Beckford's stated reason for expanding into No. 19 was that he did not want noisy neighbours. His plan was to leave it empty, but having acquired it he could not resist moving in. He proceeded to instal the sumptuous library which still exists on the ground floor, and to introduce a strange tunnel-like staircase. He filled the houses with works of art, both paintings and *objets*. Slowly, after all the years of being a social outcast, he was accepted back into society, in, of all places, solid, respectable Bath. He became friendly with the Unitarian minister Jerom Murch, who was seven times Mayor of Bath, and he met Brunel, who was busy socializing in an attempt to win friends to promote his plans for the Clifton Suspension Bridge.

Beckford continued to extend his holdings up the hill, sometimes buying but mainly leasing. Part of the estate was laid out as gardens, with Hamilton's kitchen garden fully refurbished, the hothouses and melon pits restored and the terraces used for espalier fruit. Another kitchen garden was laid out at the top of the hill, in an old quarry. Various structures were erected, such as the Embattled Gateway

overlooking the lower kitchen garden and an Italianate villa, created out of an old cottage, in the upper kitchen garden. He leased a farm, Charlcombe Field Farm, from the Gunnings. At the summit of the hill, an old quarry was turned into a nature reserve. Managing a wild area to make an effective reserve is considered a modern idea, but Beckford did it in the nineteenth century. He had been anti-hunting since his days at Fonthill, building a wall around the estate to prevent the hunt entering. In his new estate at Bath he planted shrubs and even brambles and nettles to attract the right kind of wildlife. Few landlords would have gone to such lengths to provide nesting habitat for nightingales, and he was rewarded by the pleasure of hearing them sing.

Finally, on the top of the windswept down, he built a tower. The architect was Goodridge, but most of the designing seems to have been done by Beckford himself. It appears that originally Beckford had planned the tower to be shorter than it is now. He added what is known as the Belvidere

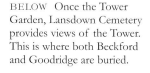

BELOW Once the Tower Garden, Lansdown Cemetery provides views of the Tower. This is where both Beckford and Goodridge are buried.

(Beckford's spelling) and then decided to go on again and top it with its crowning glory, the Lantern, based on the Choragic Monument of Lysicrates in Athens. A passage in his travel diaries, published in 1783, suggests what may have been the origin of his idea for the tower. He had visited Venice when he was just twenty, and wrote of his delight in running up the campanile, taking in the views and breathing the fresh air. 'Such an interesting combination of objects, such regal scenery, with the reflection that many of their ornaments once contributed to the decoration of Athens, transported me beyond myself,' he wrote. His tower in Bath was filled with works of art, but, more importantly, he could once again climb to its summit, breathe the fresh air, and enjoy 'the finest view in Europe'. Perhaps he imagined himself as the Caliph in his novel *Vathek*, who made himself feel godlike by seeing the world looking so small beneath him. If so, it was an experience that many wanted to share. Princess Victoria visited the tower during her visit to Bath in

1830. Brunel came a few months later, subsequently adapting its design for the pumping towers on his atmospheric railway in Devon.

The Bath to which Beckford came in 1823 still attracted aristocratic visitors, even if many of them were impoverished or elderly. By his death in 1844, Bath was becoming a backwater. Although the railway had come to Bath, allowing greater numbers of visitors to arrive quickly and cheaply, most preferred to go elsewhere. Wild mountainous areas and seaside resorts were becoming increasingly accessible, and it was to these places that visitors were going in increasing numbers. Moreover, improvements in medicine meant that Bath's waters were no longer recommended by doctors as the first line of treatment. Increasingly, Bath became a place of retirement for the elderly and of tuition for the young. John Wesley's school, originally founded at Kingswood near Bristol, moved to Lansdown, as did the Royal School for the Daughters of

BELOW At the top of his Tower, fenced by gilded railings, Beckford could emulate his anti-hero Vathek, gazing godlike on the world far below.

LEFT The cantilevered spiral staircase which climbs up to the Belvidere. Beckford's original colour scheme has been restored.

BELOW The gilded columns of the Lantern, based on the Choragic Monument of Lysicrates in Athens.

LEFT AND RIGHT Scenes
from the Cotswold Way. It runs
over a distance of more than a
hundred miles from Chipping
Campden to Bath, passing the
Lansdown racecourse and
Prospect Stile before descending
by a track to Weston and hence
into Bath.

PAGES 202–203 A final
view of Bath in evening sunshine.
From the Skyline Walk on the
south, we look across the city, the
Abbey at its heart, to the slopes
of Lansdown. Here we can
reflect on all the changes that
have come to this valley as time,
and the hot springs, flowed on.

Army Officers, which took over the premises of an earlier school, the short-lived Bath and Lansdown Proprietary College. Both were designed by the architect James Wilson, who lived on Lansdown and is responsible for many of the villas on Lansdown Road.

Beckford's Tower still looks over open countryside but there are further points of interest as we head across the down. Chapel Farm is so-called because it lay on an ancient route used by pilgrims travelling to Glastonbury. The farmhouse shows remnants of Gothic tracery. This is all that remains of the medieval hospital or hospice with its adjoining chapel dedicated to St Lawrence.

Near by is the racecourse, established here in 1784, when it moved from Claverton Down. It was described as having the finest turf in the kingdom, besides being 'convenient to the gentlemen of Bristol and Gloucestershire etc'. By 1795 it was in decline, but was revived in 1811, although a visitor eight years later described the grandstand as 'a very mean and contemptible erection . . . which is nothing more than an empty shed thatched over'. He went on to say that at race meetings there were frequent prosecutions against those caught 'badger-baiting, pricking in the garter or practising any other nefarious games'. Such games would never be found at today's Bath races, which are far more respectable, with a large grandstand rather than a thatched shed. Even

this is not considered good enough, and there are plans to redevelop the site completely.

Anyone walking the Cotswold Way, a route of over a hundred miles which travels north from Bath to Chipping Campden, will pass Granville's Monument, erected to commemorate the death of the leader of the Royalist forces at the Battle of Lansdown. Standing beside it in bright sunlight, it is hard to believe that men fought and died here, on the edge of these steep slopes.

Twenty-first-century Bath has various industries, including light engineering, computer software, printing and publishing. The two universities have brought a lively new population of students. Yet, whether Bath likes it or not, it is the precarious industry of tourism that is still at the heart of the city's economy. External events and new fashions in holiday destinations affect the city just as much now as they did in the eighteenth century. It is in Bath's favour that the trend towards complementary medicine has reawakened interest in water cures. The new Thermae Bath Spa aims to cater for visitors from all over the world who want to avail themselves of Bath's waters, whether for health or for pleasure. At last the springs, unused for thirty years, can once again bring prosperity. As long as the hot springs run the magic will remain for all those who live, work and play in the city of Bath.

INDEX

RECOMMENDED READING

In a book of this length I have only been able to touch on many matters that readers may wish to follow up in greater depth. I hope this list of recommended reading, together with some useful websites, will help them to do so. A copy of the full bibliography can be obtained from Bath & North East Somerset Record Office, Guildhall, High Street, Bath BA1 5AW.

FICTION

Two of Jane Austen's books, *Northanger Abbey* and *Persuasion*, have important scenes set in Bath. Tobias Smollett's *Humphry Clinker* and Charles Dickens's *Pickwick Papers* provide other views of the city.

NON-FICTION

ROMAN BATH   Professor Barry Cunliffe's book *Roman Bath Discovered*, published in 2000 by Tempus (Brimscombe, Gloucestershire), remains one of the most authoritative books on the archaeological work carried out in Bath, although some theories have changed in the light of more recent excavations. Bath Archaeological Trust has an informative website www.batharchaeology.org.uk which contains news of the latest projects. The Roman Baths Museum website www.romanbaths.co.uk gives the history of the baths, together with details of the Peregrinus project, a virtual journey across Roman Europe.

MEDIEVAL BATH   Peter Davenport's book *Medieval Bath Uncovered*, published in 2002 by Tempus, is an absolute requirement for those interested in this period, taking the reader from Saxon times to the Tudors. The website www.building-history.pwp.blueyonder.co.uk, run by historian Jean Manco, also contains a great deal of information about Saxon and medieval Bath.

SEVENTEENTH CENTURY   Little is readily available on this period. Celia Fiennes commented on the city in her usual vivid style, and her journal, published in various editions as *The Journeys of Celia Fiennes*, is well worth reading. *A Community at War, The Civil War in Bath and North Somerset, 1642–1650*, by local historian John Wroughton, published by Lansdown Press (Bath) in 1992, gives a good description of the city in those troubled times.

GEORGIAN BATH TO THE PRESENT DAY   The best source of information on Georgian Bath is John Wood's *An Essay towards a Description of Bath* but this is now a rare book, usually only available for consultation in libraries. Walter Ison's *Georgian Buildings of Bath* (Bath Preservation Trust, 1996), is not reliable as a history, but his architectural descriptions remain unsurpassed. A broader and more up-to-date view is offered by a new version of the *Pevsner Architectural Guide to Bath,* by Michael Forsyth (Yale University Press, New Haven and London, 2004). R.S Neale's *Bath: A Social History 1680–1850* (Routledge and Kegan Paul, London, 1981), sadly now out of print, is a detailed study of how and why Bath changed during those years. Also out of print but well worth tracking down is *John Wood, Architect of Obsession* by Tim Mowl and Brian Earnshaw (Millstream Books, Bath, 1988) a lively and controversial view of a man who himself was no stranger to controversy. Susan Sloman's *Gainsborough in Bath* (Yale University Press, 2002) not only tells the story of the artist but also contains some interesting observations about the city. The series called Bath History contains well-researched essays by various writers. Bath Archaeological Trust now oversees this project, and its website contains a full list of all the articles. An interesting study of Bath's image in the media is *The Image of Georgian Bath, 1700–2000* by Peter Borsay (Oxford University Press, 2000). Although there are some parts of this book with which I disagree, it is a thought-provoking work and Borsay's comments should be borne in mind when reading other books on Bath. Finally, a great deal of hitherto neglected history, ancient and modern, is contained in *Bath Pubs* by Andrew Swift and Kirsten Elliott (Akeman Press, Bath, 2003).

ACKNOWLEDGEMENTS

I would like to thank everyone who has helped and encouraged me with this book. The Archivist Colin Johnson and his assistants Lucy Powell and Mary Blagdon at the Guildhall have, as ever, been a source of help and guidance. The staff in Bath Central Library have also spent considerable time and effort tracking down documents and books from the depths of the local store.

To anyone trying to write a history of Bath which covers more than life in the eighteenth century, the work of Bath Archaeological Trust is invaluable. I would particularly like to thank Marek Lewcun. His enthusiastic campaign to keep local residents informed about the latest archaeological discoveries has provided me not only with much of my information about Aquae Sulis, but also an object lesson in how to make history come alive. Meanwhile, Peter Davenport's book on medieval Bath has shed new light on centuries which have long been neglected in general books about the city. It has been my principal source when writing about this period. Neil Jackson kindly shared his research on the convoluted family tree of the Pulteney family and their descendants, and explained the significance of the coat of arms in Great Pulteney Street

Some of the research has been by Dr Andrew Swift, who also read through the text. I am grateful for his criticism, which has been most constructive, whether relating to factual content or to literary style.

Finally, I would like to thank all those people who have shared their reminiscences, thoughts and ideas with me. Many are Bathonians who remember a city long gone, and others are, like me, incomers who have fallen in love with this unique city and its history.